100 AMERICAN WOMEN
WHO SHAPED AMERICAN HISTORY

DEBORAH G. FELDER

sourcebooks
eXplore

T0014539

Published by Sourcebooks eXplore, an imprint of Sourcebooks Kids
P.O. Box 4410, Naperville, Illinois 6056-410
(630) 961-3900
sourcebookskids.com

Originally published in 2005 by Bluewood Books, a division of The Siyeh Group, Inc.

Cataloging-in-Publication Data is on file with the Library of Congress.

Source of Production: Versa Press, East Peoria, Illinois, USA
Date of Production: September 2023
Trade Paperback ISBN: 9781728290119 Run Number: 5033346
Hardcover ISBN: 9781728290126 Run Number: 5033347

Printed and bound in the United States of America.
VP 10 9 8 7 6 5 4 3 2 1

CONTENTS

1   2   3 4 5   7   15
                           6 8 9 10 11 12 13 14 16 17 18 19 20 21

Timeline of Birthdates

1590   1860

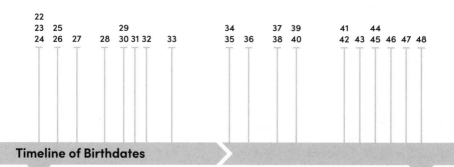

22
23 25 29 34 37 39 41 44
24 26 27 28 30 31 32 33 35 36 38 40 42 43 45 46 47 48

Timeline of Birthdates

1860

1900

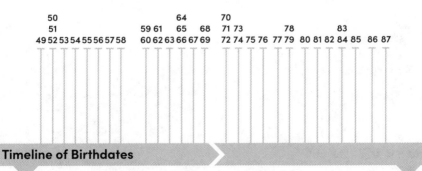

Timeline of Birthdates

1900

1950

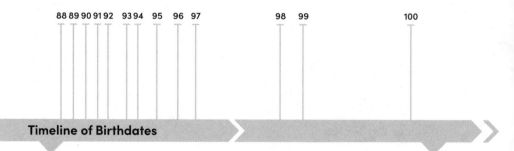

88 89 90 91 92   93 94   95   96   97   98   99   100

Timeline of Birthdates

1950   2000

INTRODUCTION

THIS BOOK contains the stories of one hundred extraordinary American women whose outstanding contributions have shaped our history from colonial times to the present day. Many of the women whose biographies are described in these pages are so famous that it is no surprise to find them in a book titled *100 American Women Who Shaped American History*. Others may be less well-known, but their stories are no less compelling.

Many of the women you will read about endured poverty, racism, sexism, and other obstacles in their struggle to succeed, yet despite these structural inequities, they were determined to reach their goals.

These women transformed their lives, and in so doing, they had a major impact and influence on their country and the lives of the women who followed them.

The experiences of American women are as diverse as the nation we have become. However, the women featured in this book had one thing in common: they were willing to challenge society's traditional, often male-dominated notions of gender, class, politics, economics, and culture.

Sometimes the cost of rebellion was high. During the colonial era, the Massachusetts government banished Puritan leader Anne Hutchinson from the colony for breaking a law that forbade women from preaching. In the nineteenth century, journalist Nellie Bly revealed the poor conditions of female prisoners after being arrested herself. In the early twentieth century, at a time when providing information on contraception was illegal, Margaret Sanger was also arrested after opening a birth control clinic.

Women have always fought for change. In the mid-nineteenth century, abolitionist sisters Sarah and Angelina Grimké spoke out publicly against slavery. During the nineteenth and early twentieth centuries, social reformers and activists such as Frances Willard, Florence Kelley, Rose Schneiderman, and Eleanor Roosevelt worked to better conditions for women in society and in the workplace.

Better education for girls and women became a reality thanks to the efforts of educators and activists like Emma Willard and Sarah Josepha Hale. The battle for women's suffrage was finally won because of the contributions of Belva Ann Lockwood, Julia Ward Howe, and Alice Paul. In the 1950s and 1960s, Septima Poinsette Clark, Ella Baker, and Mamie Till were at the forefront of the Civil Rights Movement.

The achievements of American women in such areas as the arts, government, aviation, science, and sports have been remarkable. From composer Florence Price to novelist Edith Wharton, American women artists have influenced the ways in which we see the world. Supreme Court Justice Sandra Day O'Connor and Secretary of State Madeleine Albright were two of the first women to reach the highest levels of government. Jacqueline Cochran, Mae Jemison, and Sally Ride inspired young women to seek careers in aviation and space flight.

Our understanding of disease, genetics, the environment, and computers has been transformed by the work of such scientists as Gertrude B. Elion, Florence Bascom, and Patricia Bath. In addition, Billie Jean King, Althea Gibson, and Simone Biles defied gender and racial stereotyping to become world-class athletes.

These are only some of the many inspiring women whose stories make up this book. As you scan through the various biographies or read each individual entry, one thing will become clear—American women began to shape history from the birth of the nation and have continued doing so for centuries.

Challenging the rigid **Puritan** religious doctrine of sixteenth-century New England was a courageous and risky undertaking, especially for a woman. However, **ANNE HUTCHINSON** was willing to risk everything she had for **religious freedom**.

Born in Alford, Lincolnshire, England, Anne was the second of thirteen children of Francis Marbury, an Anglican clergyman. Marbury's open-mindedness and dislike of authority constantly set him at odds with the strict religious establishment. Anne learned religious doctrine from her father and would later show that she had inherited his independent spirit.

In 1612, Anne married **William Hutchinson**, a well-to-do businessman. The couple lived in Alford, where Anne gave birth to twelve of their fifteen children. There she came under the influence of **John Cotton**, an Anglican minister who followed the Puritan sect. When the Anglican authorities condemned Cotton for his beliefs and forced him to flee to the Puritan-dominated **Massachusetts Bay Colony**, Anne convinced her husband that they should follow him there.

The Hutchinsons arrived in Boston in 1634. William prospered in the cloth trade and was a deputy to the colony's General Court. Anne's brilliant mind, gentle nature, and nursing skills won her the admiration of prominent Boston women. While tending to them, Anne discovered that her beliefs differed from the established Puritan doctrine on which the colony's society was based.

This doctrine, the "**covenant of works**," held that salvation could be achieved through hard work, good deeds, and righteous behavior.

Anne believed in a "**covenant of grace**," in which salvation lay in an individual's personal faith in God and could be obtained without relying on the help of a minister or priest.

Anne began to hold weekly meetings for women to discuss scripture and church sermons, and she also started to preach her unique beliefs. She criticized the traditional teachings by Puritan leaders. The meetings grew into large public gatherings attended by men and women, including some of Boston's leading families.

Governor **John Winthrop** and other Puritan leaders were enraged by this threat to their authority. They banned Anne's meetings and dismissed William Hutchinson from his government posts. However, Anne defied the authorities and continued to preach.

In 1637, the authorities charged her with heresy and sedition, and brought her before the General Court. The Court found her guilty and banished her and her family from Massachusetts.

In 1638, the Hutchinsons, together with thirty-five other families, went to **Rhode Island**, where they purchased land from the Narragansett people and started a democratic community. After William Hutchinson's death in 1642, Anne and her children moved to Pelham Bay, New York. There, in 1643, she and most of her children were attacked and killed by American Indian Siwanoy warriors.

ANNE BRADSTREET was the first published poet in America and the first significant woman writer in the American colonies.

Born in Northampton, England, she was the first daughter and the second of five children of Thomas and Dorothy Dudley. Her father held a prestigious and well-paying position as steward of the earl of Lincoln's vast estates, and her mother hailed from a wealthy family. Anne was educated by private tutors and supplemented her learning by reading books from the earl's well-stocked library. She was brought up in a strict religious household that did not observe the established Church of England, and instead followed a Protestant doctrine that was closer to **Puritanism**.

At the age of sixteen, Anne Dudley was married to **Simon Bradstreet**, who succeeded her father as steward. In 1630 Anne, her husband, and her parents sailed for New England on board one of Governor John Winthrop's ships. Because her father and husband were associated with the Massachusetts Bay Company, the organization that had established the **Massachusetts Bay Colony**, Anne enjoyed a position of honor and dignity in Boston. In 1644, the Bradstreets moved to North Andover, then an area of wilderness north of Boston.

Anne Bradstreet wrote poems for her own pleasure, and they were copied for her father and family members to read. In her early poems, she imitated the style of European writers, but she later found her own form of expression. At the same time, she was raising eight children, battling frequent illnesses, and keeping house in the wilderness.

In 1650, her poems were printed in a collection titled *The Tenth Muse Lately Sprung Up In America.* Anne wrote about her new life in America and her feelings on religion, nature, home, and family. Her poems provide valuable insights into seventeenth-century Puritan life and are noteworthy for their authenticity and simple beauty.

Subsequently, her brother-in-law, Reverend **John Woodbridge**, obtained a copy of Anne's early poems without her knowledge or consent, and had them printed in London to elevate the image of devout women as mothers and wives.

A second volume of poetry, *Several Poems Compiled With Great Variety of Wit and Learning,* was published six years after Anne's death. The work included revisions of her early work as well as later poems that revealed her maturity as a poet. A prose piece, "Meditations Divine and Moral," written for her son Simon, was discovered after her death. Other unpublished writings may have been destroyed in a fire at her home in 1666.

Anne Bradstreet died in North Andover. Her burial place is not known, and no portrait of her is known to exist. Among her distinguished descendants are writer **Richard Henry Dana** and U.S. Supreme Court Justice **Oliver Wendell Holmes Jr**.

As the wife of General **George Washington**, **MARTHA WASHINGTON** brought comfort and hope to the soldiers of the Continental Army during the darkest days of the **Revolutionary War**. As the first **First Lady** of the United States, she was a role model for all first ladies who followed her.

The oldest of eight children of John and Frances Dandridge, Martha Washington was born and raised on a Virginia plantation. Like most well-to-do girls of the time, she received an education that would prepare her to manage a household. At nineteen, she married **Daniel Parke Custis**, a plantation owner twenty years her senior. The couple had four children, two of whom died in infancy. Daniel Custis died in 1757, leaving the twenty-six-year-old Martha a very wealthy widow with an 18,000-acre estate to manage.

In 1758, George Washington, then a thirty-six-year-old colonel and commander of the Virginia militia, began to court Martha. On January 6, 1759, they were married at her home. The couple, together with Martha's son and daughter, went to live at **Mount Vernon**, Washington's plantation. There, Martha looked after the large household, oversaw the dairy and smokehouse, and supervised the estate's spinning and weaving center.

When Washington was named commander in chief of the Continental Army in 1775, Martha joined him at his headquarters near Boston. From that time until the Revolutionary War was over, she spent the winters with Washington at the army's encampments. Her calm, steady, and cheerful spirit was a great comfort to her husband and the soldiers, especially at **Valley Forge** during the harsh winter of 1778, when it seemed that the war would be lost. She nursed sick and wounded soldiers, mended their clothes, made shirts, and knitted socks for them. She also encouraged other military wives to join her.

In 1789, George Washington became the first president of the United States, and Martha and two of her four grandchildren accompanied him to the new nation's first capital, New York City. There was debate over what to call Martha; with some people addressing her as "Lady Washington." However, she preferred to hear just "Mrs. Washington." She gave formal dinner parties at the presidential home, appeared with the president on ceremonial occasions, and hosted weekly Friday evening receptions with **Abigail Adams** (see no. 4), wife of Vice President John Adams. Martha created an elegant atmosphere surrounding the presidency, and her friendly but dignified manner soon made her a popular public figure.

After Washington's two terms in office, he and his wife retired to Mount Vernon. George Washington died in 1799. Martha Washington lived quietly at Mount Vernon for the next two years and died there at the age of seventy-one.

4 ABIGAIL ADAMS
1744–1818

The nation's second **First Lady**, **ABIGAIL ADAMS** was an unusual woman for her time. Ambitious for herself as well as for her husband, she was highly opinionated and did not hesitate to speak out on political and social issues. She believed in the equal status of women and most importantly, in a woman's right to a good education.

Born in Weymouth, Massachusetts, Abigail Adams was the second of four children of the Reverend William Smith and Elizabeth Smith. Abigail was a frail child and in poor health all her life. She was educated by her parents and spent her childhood reading Shakespeare and classical literature. She also taught herself French.

On October 25, 1764, nineteen-year-old Abigail wed twenty-nine-year-old lawyer **John Adams**, beginning an extraordinarily happy marriage that would last until Abigail's death. The couple lived in **Braintree**, a town outside of Boston, on a farm that John had inherited. They had five children, four of whom survived to adulthood. The eldest son, **John Quincy Adams** (1767–1848), would become the sixth U.S. president.

In 1774, John Adams went to Philadelphia when he was elected to the Massachusetts delegation to the First Continental Congress. For the next ten years, except for very brief visits, the Adamses would live apart, while John served his country in Philadelphia and France. In his absence, Abigail educated the children, managed the household and the farm, hired the household staff, and paid the bills. A capable and prudent businesswoman, she successfully carried out all these responsibilities during the Revolutionary War, when the economy was disrupted and provisions were scarce.

One of the great letter writers of all time, she is known for her famous letters to Adams, whom she addressed as "Dearest Friend."

While they were separated, Abigail wrote to him at least once a day. Her letters included day-to-day information on the family and the farm, war news, and political insights.

During the eight years of John Adams's vice-presidency (1789–1797) and four years of his presidency (1797–1801), Abigail moved back and forth between Braintree and the capitals in New York City and Philadelphia.

During the last three months of Adams's term, Abigail and John moved to the new capital, Washington, to live in the unfinished President's House. The executive mansion was so cold and damp that Abigail kept fires going in the mansion's thirteen fireplaces twenty-four hours a day. She hung the family's laundry in what is now the East Room of the White House.

After John Adams lost the 1800 U.S. presidential election to Thomas Jefferson, the Adamses returned to Braintree. There, Abigail enjoyed seventeen quiet years as the matriarch of her large family. She became ill with a fever in October 1818 and died shortly afterward.

This **Philadelphia seamstress** is celebrated for creating the first Stars and Stripes—the **American flag** we know and honor today. However, is the story about **BETSY ROSS** and the flag fact or fiction? The truth has long been a subject of debate.

Betsy Ross was born Elizabeth Griscom in Philadelphia, one of seventeen children of Samuel Griscom, a carpenter and a **Quaker**. Her mother, Rebecca, taught her needlework. In 1773, Betsy married **John Ross**, an upholsterer's apprentice. John was an Anglican, and because Betsy had married outside her faith, she was expelled from the Quaker community. However, she later joined the **Free Quakers**, a more tolerant sect.

The Rosses started an upholstery business, but in January 1776, John was killed in a gunpowder explosion while on militia duty at the Philadelphia waterfront. Betsy continued to run the business and supplemented her income by making flags for the colony of Pennsylvania. She became well off enough to purchase property in Philadelphia and the Pennsylvanian countryside.

According to popular legend, in June 1776 or 1777, **George Washington** and other members of a secret committee of the Continental Congress came to the upholstery shop to ask Betsy to design a flag for the new nation. They showed her a rough sketch with six-pointed stars, but when she demonstrated how easy it would be for her to cut five-pointed stars out of cloth, they accepted her design and commissioned her to make the flag. In some versions of the story, Betsy received a contract to make flags for the government and continued to manufacture them until her death.

Betsy married twice after John Ross's death. Her second husband, whom she wed in 1777, was **Joseph Ashburn**, a ship's first mate. The couple had two daughters. In 1781, during the **Revolutionary War**, the British captured Ashburn's ship. Ashburn died in an English prison two years later. In 1783, Betsy married **John Claypoole**, a friend of Ashburn's and a fellow prisoner. Betsy and John Claypoole had five daughters. Claypoole died in 1817. Betsy remained in Philadelphia until her death at the age of eighty-four.

Although historical records show a payment to "Elizabeth Ross" in 1777 for making flags, there is no solid evidence that she sewed the first flag. However, the story of Betsy and the flag was passed down in her family. In 1870, Betsy's grandson, **William Canby**, presented his essay about the story at a meeting of the Historical Society of Pennsylvania. The story made its way into magazines and books, and by the 1880s, it was in school textbooks. Today, the Betsy Ross House in Philadelphia, where she allegedly sewed the Stars and Stripes, is a national museum.

In her satin dresses and trademark-feathered turbans, **DOLLEY MADISON** brought glamour to Washington. And her bravery and patriotism during a time of war later earned her a reputation as one of America's most courageous **first ladies**.

Born Dorothea Payne in North Carolina and raised on a plantation near Ashland, Virginia, she was the eldest daughter of nine children. Her **Quaker** parents, John and Mary, doted on her and gave her the nickname "Dolley."

In 1790, she married **John Todd, Jr.**, a young Quaker lawyer, who died three years later while caring for victims of a yellow fever epidemic in Philadelphia. Dolley and her sons, a two-year-old and a newborn, also became ill. She and her older son survived, but the infant died. In 1794, after a four-month courtship, Dolley married Virginia congressman, **James Madison**.

The Quakers disowned Dolley because she had married outside her faith. This meant that she was freed from their restrictions and could attend social functions that the Quakers had frowned upon, such as balls and receptions.

In 1801, President **Thomas Jefferson** appointed Madison his secretary of state. Since both Jefferson and his vice president, Aaron Burr, were widowers, Dolley, as the wife of the highest-ranking Cabinet official, hosted presidential dinners and receptions. She carried out her duties with warmth, wit, and charm—a pattern she would continue after her husband was elected president in 1808.

During Madison's presidency, Dolley produced a social whirlwind at the White House. The executive mansion became a virtually endless succession of dinner parties, lawn parties, luncheons, and dances.

While she was always dressed in the most glamorous fashions of the day, Dolley was known for having the talent to inject into the most formal occasions the informal gaiety of a country dance or an intimate tea party among friends.

Dolley became a heroine during the **War of 1812**. In August 1814, with her husband away at the front and British troops fast approaching the White House, Dolley managed to save the famous Gilbert Stuart portrait of George Washington and other valuables before fleeing to safety in Virginia. The British burned down the executive mansion, and it would not be fully restored until 1817 during James Monroe's presidency.

After the British retreat, the Madisons moved to another Washington residence called the **Octagon House**. There, Dolley hosted several galas to celebrate the American victory over the British in 1815.

In 1817, at the close of Madison's second term, Dolley and her husband retired to his Virginia estate. James died in 1836, and a year later, Dolley returned to Washington, where she became the capital's most popular hostess. She died of a stroke in July 1849.

The first person born in the United States to be **canonized** by the **Roman Catholic** church, **ST. ELIZABETH SETON** shaped American history by establishing **the first Catholic parochial school** in the United States.

Born Elizabeth Ann Bayley in New York City, she was the second of three daughters of prominent physician Richard Bayley, a pioneer of surgical techniques and the study of diphtheria.

When Elizabeth was three years old, her mother, Catherine, died. Her father remarried and had seven more children with his second wife, Charlotte. As a young girl, Elizabeth developed a deep love for the Psalms, which her stepmother taught to her. The family's religious background was Huguenot (French Protestant) and Episcopalian.

In 1794, at the age of nineteen, Elizabeth married **William Seton**, a prosperous young merchant. The couple had five children. In 1800, Seton's business failed, and he went bankrupt. In 1803, William Seton died in Italy, where he had journeyed with Elizabeth and one of their daughters.

In Italy, Elizabeth visited churches, and an Irish priest she met in Livorno introduced her to the teachings of the Roman Catholic Church. In 1804, she returned to New York, and the following year she converted to Catholicism. She was confirmed in 1806.

Because of her conversion, her godmother disinherited her, and she encountered hostility from many of her Protestant friends and relatives. Faced with the need to support herself and her children, she tried unsuccessfully to start a school in Albany, New York, and then ran a boarding house for boys who attended an Episcopal school.

In 1808, Reverend **William Dubourg** invited Elizabeth to Baltimore, Maryland, to start a school for Catholic girls called the **Paca Street School**. There, she taught the daughters of prominent Catholic families and prepared them for their First Communion. The same year, she founded a religious community in Emmitsburg, Maryland, which would become a new religious order known as the **Sisters of Charity of St. Joseph**.

After this, she was called **Mother Seton**, and she took her first vows as a nun in 1809. The community grew rapidly and included St. Joseph Academy for girls from prosperous families. The income from her boarders allowed Mother Seton to offer free schooling for needy Catholic girls from the local parish.

This marked the beginning of the parochial school system in the United States. Mother Seton became the superior of her Order, which in her lifetime, grew to include communities in Philadelphia (1814) and New York (1817). The Sisters of Charity would eventually grow to twenty communities with schools, orphanages, and hospitals. Mother Seton died of tuberculosis at the age of forty-six. She was beatified in 1963 and canonized in 1975.

Emigrating from the United States to Canada as a child, **ROSE FORTUNE** is considered a trailblazing Black female entrepreneur with strong character and unshakable spirit. She developed two successful businesses and carved out her own space in a time and place when opportunity was scarce.

Rose Fortune was born in Philadelphia, Pennsylvania, around 1774, to enslaved parents. After the **Revolutionary War** began, her parents became **Black Loyalists**—people of African descent who declared loyalty to the British during the war in exchange for their freedom. Like many Black Loyalists, Rose's family crossed British Army lines and emigrated to Canada, presumably around 1783.

Not much is known about Rose's early life in Canada, but in early adulthood she made a name for herself as a pragmatic entrepreneur. During a time when Black people and women were still facing regular discrimination in Canada, Rose built a reputation for herself as a successful woman in business. Seeing a need for materials transport services for the luggage and supplies on incoming ships, she developed a baggage handling business, moving items in a wheelbarrow from local wharves to the inns and hotels. At the start, she used wheelbarrows to transfer items, but eventually her business grew to use horse-drawn wagons. Having established a business that required her to travel between the wharves and town, she eventually expanded her services and began issuing warnings to visitors at inns who were about to miss their departing ships.

Rose was well-known among the townspeople as a woman who made her own way in the world, was not afraid to speak her mind, and kept other people in line when necessary. She protected her business pursuits fiercely, and she often reprimanded young men who attempted to encroach on her business. Through her unabashed confrontational skills, Rose became known as a kind of unofficial police officer around town, most famously known for enforcing curfews at the wharves.

Historical records show Rose had at least three children. Although she died on February 20, 1864, she left an impressive legacy for her family and fellow Black Loyalists. Her grandchildren and great-grandchildren carried on her businesses over the next century, and many of her descendants still work in the shipping industry today. For those struggling to make a name for themselves in the face of adversity, Rose was a role model who rose to success through perseverance and staying true to herself.

A pioneer educator, **EMMA WILLARD** established the **Troy Female Seminary**, the first school to offer collegiate education to women and new opportunities for women teachers.

Emma Hart was born and raised on a farm in Berlin, Connecticut, the second youngest of seventeen children. She grew up in an era when women were thought to be intellectually inferior to men, but her father Samuel Hart encouraged her to not accept that view. At thirteen, she taught herself geometry, and in 1802, she enrolled at the **Berlin Academy**. By 1804, she began teaching the academy's youngest children.

By 1807, she was employed as the head of a girl's school in Middlebury, Vermont. Two years later, she married **John Willard**, a physician nearly thirty years her senior. The couple had a son named John Hart Willard in 1810. To help support her family, Emma founded the **Middlebury Female Academy** in 1814. She held classes at the Willard home, teaching her students subjects not then available to girls, such as mathematics, science, and classic literature. The school's success inspired her to expand, and she envisioned a program of state-aided schools for girls in neighboring New York State.

In 1819, she petitioned Governor DeWitt Clinton and the New York State Legislature for funds, and she wrote a pamphlet titled *A Plan for Improving Female Education*, which persuasively argued for a woman's right to receive an education. However, her request was rejected by the legislature.

In 1821, the town of Troy, New York, raised $4,000 for Willard to establish a school there. In September, she opened the Troy Female Seminary, which began with ninety students. Willard developed the courses and teaching methods, and she wrote many of the textbooks for the seminary's classes. The curriculum was unique in that it featured college-level courses previously only taught in schools exclusively for men. At the time, the school offered the most advanced curriculum for young women in the entire United States. By 1823, the Troy Female Seminary had educated two hundred women teachers, who spread Willard's teaching methods throughout the country.

Willard's husband had died in 1825. In 1838, Willard turned over management of the seminary to her son and daughter-in-law, and she married another physician named **Christopher Yates**. The couple lived in Connecticut, where Willard worked to improve the school system. Yates proved to be a gambler and a scoundrel, and Willard divorced him in 1843. The following year, she moved back to Troy to be near the seminary. She spent the rest of her life teaching, speaking, and writing on educational subjects as well as helping to form educational societies. In 1895, the Troy Female Seminary was renamed the **Emma Willard School**.

When a well-dressed woman wanted to see the latest fashions in the mid-1800s, she consulted *Godey's Lady's Book*. The lavishly illustrated periodical was the most popular magazine of its day, and for nearly four decades, its editor was **SARAH JOSEPHA HALE**—the first woman to edit a major American magazine. She also wrote and edited some fifty books, and authored one of the most famous poems of all time, "Mary Had a Little Lamb."

Born Sarah Buell in Newport, New Hampshire, Hale was the second youngest child in a family of two sons and two daughters. She was educated at home by her mother, Martha, and her older brother, Horatio, a student at Dartmouth College. From 1806 to 1813, Sarah operated a school for the children of Newport. In 1813, she married lawyer **David Hale**, who died of pneumonia in 1822, four days before the birth of the couple's fifth child. To help support her family, she opened a millinery shop with her sister-in-law and published a novel as well as poetry books for children.

In 1827, Hale accepted a position as editor of *Ladies Magazine*, which was based in Boston. She changed the magazine's format to include original writings, rather than reprinted poems and stories. She also wrote many of the articles herself, and featured articles on such topics as family life, the household duties of women, and the importance of charity work. Although Hale was not a supporter of women's suffrage, she championed women's education and supported educators such as **Emma Willard** (see no. 9) and **Thomas Gallaudet**, a pioneer in education for the deaf.

In 1837, Philadelphia publisher **Louis Godey** bought *Ladies' Magazine*, merged it with his own publication *Godey's Lady's Book,* and retained Hale as the magazine's editor.

She held that position for nearly forty years. Under her editorship, *Godey's* became the largest magazine of its time, with a readership of more than one hundred fifty thousand by 1860. In addition to the kind of articles, poetry, and fiction that had appeared in *Ladies Magazine*, Hale included beautiful color plates of the latest fashion. Godey's also included household hints, diet and health advice, columns on married women's rights, and stories on notable women such as Elizabeth Blackwell, the first American woman doctor to graduate from medical school.

Sarah Josepha Hale was nearly ninety years old when she retired. In her final column, in December 1877, she wrote: "I bid farewell to my countrywomen, with the hope of half a century may be blessed to the furtherance of their happiness and usefulness in their Divinely appointed sphere." *Godey's Lady's Book* continued for another twenty years before ceasing publication in 1898.

The daughters of a wealthy southern enslaver, the Grimké sisters were some of the first American women to courageously speak out publicly against slavery.

While growing up in Charleston, South Carolina, **SARAH** and **ANGELINA GRIMKÉ** became increasingly horrified by the cruelty of slavery. Sarah, who taught in a Sunday school for enslaved people, defied state law by teaching her pupils to read. In 1819, while visiting Philadelphia, she became impressed by the antislavery position of the **Quakers**, and two years later, she shocked her family by moving there to join the sect.

In 1829, Angelina went to Philadelphia, joined the **Philadelphia Female Anti-Slavery Society**, and wrote a letter of support to famed abolitionist **William Lloyd Garrison**. The unexpected publication of the letter in Garrison's newspaper, *The Liberator*, publicly identified Angelina with the **abolitionist** cause. In 1836, she published an antislavery pamphlet that was destroyed by southern postmasters.

Animosity toward Angelina became so strong in the South that she was warned not to return to Charleston. At the request of the **American Anti-Slavery Society**, she moved to New York City to conduct meetings for women interested in the abolitionist movement. Next, joining her sister in New York, Sarah broke with the Quakers over their discriminatory treatment of African Americans at meetings and the Quakers' refusal to let her speak on behalf of Black members.

The Grimkés toured the North, lecturing on abolitionism and causing a sensation when they spoke to large "mixed" audiences of men and women. In 1837, after the Congregational churches denounced their behavior as "unwomanly" and "unnatural," the sisters turned their activism toward **women's rights**. They both wrote strong pamphlets asserting the right of women to speak out on moral and social issues, and to have a voice in the establishment of laws.

In 1838, Angelina married antislavery activist and noted orator **Theodore Weld**. In 1839, the Grimkés published *American Slavery As It Is: Testimony of a Thousand Witnesses,* which became a major source for **Harriet Beecher Stowe** while she wrote *Uncle Tom's Cabin.* By 1840, the Grimké sisters had largely retired from public life. Angelina was frequently ill, and Sarah helped raise her three children.

During the 1850s, the Welds and Sarah Grimké lived in New Jersey, where they ran a girls' boarding school. In 1862, they settled in the Boston area, where they taught at a girls' school. In 1868, the sisters learned that their brother had fathered two sons with an enslaved woman. They welcomed both young men into their home and gave them aid and encouragement. Their nephews, **Archibald Henry Grimké** and **Freeman Jones Grimké**, would go on to become prominent **civil rights activists** and spokespeople for African Americans.

A mid-nineteenth century writer, editor, critic, philosopher, and advocate for women's rights, **MARGARET FULLER** demonstrated that women could play a central role in addressing the philosophical, moral, and social issues of the day. In an age in which women, like children, were meant to be seen and not heard, Fuller was a distinctive exception, an independent thinker and writer who refused to be constrained by narrow gender roles.

Born in Cambridge, Massachusetts, Margaret Fuller was the firstborn child of a prominent Boston lawyer and politician who responded to his disappointment over having a daughter rather than a son by educating Fuller as if she was a boy. She studied subjects that were considered beyond a young girl's capabilities at the time. By the age of seven, she was reading in Latin and was given the run of her father's library. She would later go on to master French, Italian, and Greek.

When she was in her twenties, Fuller became a teacher and a member of an intellectual circle that included the noted writer and philosopher **Ralph Waldo Emerson**. In 1839, she hosted a series of famous conversations, which were gatherings for notable women of Boston to discuss art, ethics, education, and the role of women in society. The following year, she collaborated with Emerson and others to establish one of America's first great magazines, *The Dial*, which she edited until 1842.

In 1844, **Horace Greeley**, publisher of the *New York Tribune*, who regarded Fuller as "the most remarkable and in some respects the greatest woman whom America has yet known," hired her as the paper's **literary critic**, a unique achievement for a woman at the time.

The following year, Fuller published *Woman in the Nineteenth Century*, in which she explored the status of women. Regarded as an American classic, the book played an influential role in shaping the early struggle for women's rights in the United States.

In 1846, she became the *Tribune's* foreign correspondent, and the next year, she traveled to Italy to report on the revolution there. While in Italy, she met and married the young Roman nobleman **Giovanni Angelo Marchese Ossoli**, with whom she had a son. The family was returning to America in 1850 when their ship ran aground in a heavy storm a few hours outside of the New York Harbor. After a harrowing twelve hours waiting for rescuers who never arrived, Fuller, her husband, and child drowned when the ship broke apart and sank.

Although her career was tragically cut short, Margaret Fuller is still considered one of the most influential women in American history.

Internationally famous for discovering a comet that was named for her, **astronomer** and educator **MARIA MITCHELL** was the first renowned American woman scientist. Largely self-educated, she became one of the first woman faculty members of **Vassar College**, where she taught for two decades, training several generations of women who followed her path to prominence in science and other fields.

Born on the small island of Nantucket, Massachusetts, Mitchell became fascinated with the stars while assisting her father with nightly observations of the heavens on their roof. In the early nineteenth century, Nantucket was the world's most important whaling port, and most of the island's inhabitants were seafarers who depended on the stars for navigation. She helped her father check the accuracy of the navigational instruments for the Nantucket sailing fleet in nightly tests based on stellar observation.

Mitchell taught school on Nantucket and then became the island's librarian. She spent her days reading the library's books and her nights studying the stars. "I was born of only ordinary capacity," she claimed, "but of extraordinary persistency." Her persistence paid off on the night of October 1, 1847, when she became the first person to identify a comet near Polaris (the North Star) that would come to be called **"Miss Mitchell's Comet."**

Worldwide recognition for Mitchell's discovery and achievements as an astronomer followed, including a gold medal presented to her by the king of Denmark. In 1848, she became the first woman elected to the prestigious **American Academy of Arts and Sciences**.

In 1857, a group of Boston women gave Mitchell a telescope that enabled her to make many discoveries about the nature of sunspots. In 1865, Mitchell accepted a position as director of the observatory and professor of astronomy at Vassar, a women's college in New York (later Vassar College). Despite never having received a college education, Mitchell became one of the school's most respected and admired teachers.

Mitchell ignored the traditional grading system and refused to report student absences. Instead, she urged her students to "question everything," and encouraged them to develop what she considered to be a person's most important attributes: independence and individuality.

While at Vassar, Mitchell also continued her astronomical research, concentrating on the Sun and the satellites of Saturn and Jupiter. She once traveled as far as Denver, Colorado, to observe a solar eclipse.

In 1873, Mitchell helped found the **Association for the Advancement of Women** to address the challenges faced by women in the sciences and other professions. She also served as the association's president from 1875–1876.

Mitchell retired from Vassar in 1888 and died the following year. In the early twentieth century, the **Maria Mitchell Observatory** was built next door to her birthplace in Nantucket.

JULIA WARD HOWE composed one of America's most famous patriotic songs, "**The Battle Hymn of the Republic.**" She wrote the song at the outset of the Civil War to inspire Union troops and to emphasize the moral principle behind the war: the abolition of slavery. Howe used her notoriety following the war to **promote women's suffrage, prison reform**, and **international peace**.

Born in New York City, Julia Ward was the third of six children of Samuel Ward, a wealthy banker. She was tutored at home and at private schools, and she excelled at her studies. By the age of twenty she was writing and publishing literary reviews. In 1843, she married **Samuel Gridley Howe**, a noted Boston humanitarian and teacher of the blind. The couple had five children. During the 1840s and 1850s, Julia Howe authored two volumes of poetry, plays, and a travel book. She also joined her husband in the abolitionist cause.

In 1861, while attending a military review of Union troops in Washington, DC, Howe heard soldiers singing the marching song "John Brown's Body," which celebrated the fiery abolitionist leader who had been hanged in 1859 for leading an attempted revolt by enslaved people at Harpers Ferry in Virginia (now in West Virginia). One of Howe's companions, Dr. James Freeman Clarke, a Unitarian minister, knew that Howe was a poet and urged her to write some "more appropriate" words on behalf of the Union cause for this "stirring tune." By the next morning, Howe had written all the words to "The Battle Hymn of the Republic."

The words first appeared anonymously in the *Atlantic Monthly* magazine in 1862, with Howe receiving five dollars for her contribution. Set to the tune of "John Brown's Body," the song quickly became a rallying cry for Union troops. Howe's powerful and forceful language had transformed "John Brown's Body" from a song of revenge over the death of an abolitionist leader into a hymn of sacrifice for the noble cause of ending slavery.

After the Civil War, Howe—who had become famous—wrote and lectured on international peace, proposing a Mother's Day of Peace that would inspire **Anna May Jarvis** to lobby for the creation of a national Mother's Day, established in 1914. Howe also worked for women's suffrage, helping to establish both the **New England Woman Suffrage Association (NEWSA)** and the **American Woman Suffrage Association (AWSA)**.

Following the war, Howe continued her literary career as well. She founded and edited the literary magazine *Northern Lights* and was a founder and editor of the suffrage newspaper *Women's Journal*. In 1908, Howe became the first woman elected to the **American Academy of Arts and Letters**.

EMILY DICKINSON, considered the greatest woman poet to write in the English language, ironically published a mere seven poems during her lifetime—and all of them anonymously. Only a small circle of family and friends even knew that the shy and reclusive Dickinson was a poet. No one could gauge the extent of her efforts until after her death, when 1,775 poems were discovered in a locked box in her bureau. These soul-searching explorations about life and feelings would establish Dickinson as one of the world's greatest and most innovative writers.

Emily Dickinson was one of Edward Dickinson's three children. Her father was a lawyer and the treasurer of Amherst College in western Massachusetts. She was raised in a strict, conservative household. The rebel of the family was Emily's brother Austin, also a lawyer, who married a New Yorker against his father's wishes and smuggled forbidden books of poetry and essays to his sister.

Emily was educated at **Amherst Academy** and attended **Mount Holyoke Female Seminary** for a short time. As a child and young adult, she enjoyed parties and other social activities of her New England village, but after completing her schooling, she became increasingly reclusive. She rarely left home and confined herself to a small circle of family and a few trusted friends while attending to her household responsibilities.

It is believed that Dickinson may have fallen in love with her father's law apprentice, **Benjamin Newton**, who was living with her family in 1848. He was too poor to marry and died of tuberculosis in 1853. Dickinson may also have loved the Reverend **Charles Wadsworth**. He regularly visited the family until 1862, when he moved to California. Following his departure from her life, she wrote a flood of poetry expressing a personal crisis and emotional turbulence.

In Amherst, Dickinson began to acquire a reputation as an eccentric woman. She always dressed in white and was rarely seen, even by visitors to the Dickinson home. Despite her isolation, Dickinson used her everyday, ordinary experiences for poetic and spiritual illumination. If her life was uneventful, her poems show a dramatic depth in their explorations of such subjects as God, death, love, and nature, presented in lively, witty, and ironic verses.

In 1884, Dickinson became gravely ill with what is now thought to have been a kidney ailment known as Bright's disease. She died at the age of fifty-five. One of her poems serves as a fitting testimony for this great poetic voice:

This is my letter to the world,
That never wrote to me,-
The Simple news that Nature told,
With tender majesty.
Her message is committed
To hands I cannot see,
For love of her, sweet countrymen,
Judge tenderly of me.

During her long career, attorney **BELVA ANN LOCKWOOD** helped American women lawyers obtain the same professional rights and career opportunities as men more than any other nineteenth-century reformer. In 1879, she became the first woman permitted to argue a case before the **U.S. Supreme Court**.

Born Belva Bennett on a farm in Niagara County, New York, Lockwood attended country schools until the age of fifteen, when she went to work as a teacher. In 1848, she married **Uriah McNall**, a

farmer and sawmill operator. After he died in 1853, Lockwood became the sole support of her young daughter. She resumed her teaching and found time to further her education, eventually graduating from Genesee College (later Syracuse University) with honors in 1857.

In 1866, she moved to Washington, DC, where she opened one of the earliest private coeducational schools in the capital and began to study law informally. After marrying **Ezekiel Lockwood**, a former Baptist minister, she applied for admission to three law schools—all three of which rejected her because she was a woman.

In 1871, she was finally admitted to the newly created **National University Law School**. Although Lockwood completed her studies in 1873, her diploma was not issued until she petitioned President **Ulysses S. Grant** to intercede on her behalf. Soon afterward, she was admitted to the District of Columbia Bar, which two years earlier had changed the judicial rules to allow women to practice law in the district. However, when one of Lockwood's cases came before the U.S. Court of Federal Claims, the court denied her the right to argue it.

In 1876, the Supreme Court turned down her petition to grant women the right to practice their profession before the highest courts in the nation. She immediately began to lobby Congress to pass a bill to grant women equal rights as lawyers in all the courts in the country. Congress passed the bill in 1879, the same year that Lockwood argued her case before the U.S. Supreme Court. She went on to establish a large legal practice in Washington, concentrating on protecting the rights of workers and minorities such as African Americans and American Indians.

Lockwood also worked for betterment of women's rights. She cofounded the first suffrage group in Washington, DC, and participated in drafting and presenting resolutions, petitions, and bills to Congress, which included provisions for equal pay for women government workers and the extension of property rights to women.

During the late 1880s, Lockwood began to devote herself to the cause of world peace, and in 1889, she served as a delegate to the **International Congress of Charities, Correction, and Philanthropy**.

Belva Ann Lockwood died in Washington, DC, at the age of eighty-six on May 19, 1917.

The first African American woman to receive a star route with the U.S. Post Office Department (now the U.S. Postal Service), **"STAGECOACH" MARY FIELDS** chiseled out a place for herself in post–Civil War America at a time when opportunity for Black women was scarce. Her dependability and stature led her to break barriers and enjoy freedoms many others wouldn't for decades.

Mary Fields was born into slavery in Tennessee in 1832, and she remained enslaved until the end of the **American Civil War** in 1865. Looking for new opportunities, Mary moved to the South and began working on the Mississippi River as a steamboat worker. However, within a few years, she moved on to Toledo, Ohio, where she worked as a housekeeper for the Ursuline Convent. Records show that Mary had a relationship with Mother Mary Amadeus, whose family owned Mary's family when she was younger. Mother Amadeus was moved to St. Peter's Mission in Montana, and eventually Mary followed her there.

In Cascade, Montana, Mary would make a lasting name for herself. Mary was known for rejecting racial and gender stereotypes. While working at the convent, she refused to take payment, but she did accept lodging. Although no official records exist explaining why, it is likely that Mary found freedom in being able to work and move about the town freely without restrictive work requirements, and she had been able to take on several employment opportunities at once. At the convent, she tended to the facility's garden, helped with facility maintenance, managed laundry, and also brought supplies from town to the mission. She had a strong presence at six feet tall and two hundred pounds. She was also known to have a bit of a temper, and she regularly performed hard physical labor that was typically delegated to men. She even dressed in men's clothing.

Although she worked for the convent, Mary frequented saloons and drank with men on her trips to town. Historians believe that sometime after beginning work in Montana, Mary took part in a duel, and the mission's leadership demanded that she be banned from St. Peter's.

Mary moved into the town of Cascade when she was released from the mission, and she explored other employment options. She refused to take on stereotypical roles filled by Black women at the time, such as housekeeping. At first, she attempted to run eateries in town, but the businesses failed, presumably because she gave away too many supplies for free.

However, in 1895, Mary received a star route contract from the U.S. Post Office Department, becoming the first African American woman and only second woman ever to receive such a contract. Her route took her between St. Peter's Mission and Cascade, which was thirty-four miles roundtrip. She completed the route for eight years—while in her sixties—without missing one day of work, even when she had to combat poor weather, robbers, and wildlife. Her commitment won her the nickname "Stagecoach Mary."

Mary retired from her route and established another business in town before passing away in 1914 in her early eighties.

Social reformer **FRANCES WILLARD'S** personal motto of "Do everything" accurately describes her remarkable life. Despite growing up on a farm in the Wisconsin frontier and receiving only four years of formal schooling early on, Willard became the **first woman college president** in the United States, and one of the country's leading social reformers of the late nineteenth century.

Born in Churchville, New York, Frances was the fourth of five children. In 1846, her father, a cabinet-maker and farmer, moved his family to a farm in Wisconsin Territory (now in present-day Wisconsin). Frances received very little schooling as a youngster, but she yearned for an education; she later managed to graduate from the North-Western Female College in Evanston, Illinois, in 1859, with a degree in science. In 1861, she became engaged to Methodist pastor Charles Henry Fowler, but the engagement ended after several months.

Determined to lead an independent life, Willard went to work as a schoolteacher in the country and at a succession of Methodist schools. In 1870, she was named president of the **Evanston College for Ladies**, which was absorbed by Northwestern University in 1873. She remained there as dean of women and a professor of English and art until she resigned in 1874. The same year, Chicago anti-saloon crusaders asked Willard to direct their newly formed temperance organization.

Willard had found her true calling as a temperance organizer, star speaker, and eventually, in 1879, as president of the Women's Christian Temperance Union **(WCTU)**, a position she held for nearly twenty years. The WCTU was originally formed to protest the unregulated manufacture and sale of liquor and to campaign for alcohol abstinence. Under Willard's leadership, the organization also advanced the cause of women's rights and promoted reform in many fields, including suffrage, labor laws, health and hygiene, and prison reform. On behalf of the WCTU and its reforming agenda, Willard crisscrossed the country, traveling as many as twenty thousand miles a year, inspiring women to join the WCTU and support its causes.

During her leadership of the WCTU, Willard tried to create a national women's reformist organization driven by her "Do everything" program to address the social abuses of American women wherever possible. While her attempt to link women's suffrage, prohibition, and a national political party proved to be controversial and unsuccessful, Willard has been recognized as responsible for making American women aware of the importance of social activism.

Willard wrote several articles and books during her lifetime, including *Woman and Temperance* (1883), *How to Win* (1886), and her autobiography *Glimpses of Fifty Years* (1889).

When Willard died in 1898, two thousand mourners attended her funeral, and another twenty thousand filed past her coffin as she lay in state at the Woman's Temple in Chicago, Illinois.

◆ A pioneering investigative journalist, **IDA TARBELL** is famous for her classic 1904 study of corruption in the oil industry titled *The History of the Standard Oil Company*, which led to the breakup of the Standard Oil monopoly. In this book and her other writings, Tarbell challenged the greed of the rich and powerful who had selfishly blocked American ideals of equal opportunity and social justice.

Born in Erie County, Pennsylvania, Tarbell was the daughter of a wealthy oil producer. Both parents encouraged her intellectual curiosity, and at an early age, she became a strong supporter of women's rights and careers for women outside the home. She attended **Allegheny College**, where she studied biology and graduated in 1880 as one of only five women graduates.

Tarbell spent a few years teaching and editing, and in 1891 enrolled at the Sorbonne in Paris, supporting herself by writing occasional articles for American magazines. Her work attracted the attention of **S. S. McClure**, who was starting his own magazine called *McClure's*, where he published her articles and interviews with French luminaries such as Louis Pasteur. Tarbell also wrote a series of articles on **Napoleon** and **Abraham Lincoln** that were later collected and published in book form, and which brought her national acclaim.

From 1894 to 1906, Tarbell worked as an editor for *McClure's*, which was gaining a reputation as the leading **muckraking** magazine of the day, exposing corruption in various aspects of American life. The term "muckraking" was a pejorative coined by **Theodore Roosevelt**, who compared writers like Tarbell to the "man with the muckrake" in John Bunyan's *Pilgrim's Progress*—that is, someone who stirs things up.

Tarbell's major contribution as a muckraker was her landmark study attacking John D. Rockefeller's oil trust, first published as a series of articles in *McClure's*. It documented the ways in which the giant Standard Oil Company drove independent oil producers out of business and eliminated competition. The book led to a federal government investigation into the company's practices, and its eventual breakup under the **Sherman Anti-Trust Act**.

In 1906, Tarbell and fellow muckraker **Lincoln Steffens** bought the *American Magazine*, and Tarbell turned her attention to tariffs, which she exposed as yet another way that businesses gained monopolistic control. She wrote a series of articles on tariffs for *American Magazine*, and they were published in book form in 1911 as *The Tariff in Our Times*. President Woodrow Wilson was so impressed with Tarbell's work that he appointed her as a delegate to his Industrial Conference in 1919. President Harding later named her to his Conference on Unemployment in 1921.

In 1939, Tarbell published her autobiography *All in the Day's Work*. She died on January 6, 1944, in Bridgeport, Connecticut.

Throughout American history, African Americans have endured enslavement, tumultuous wars, and persistent discrimination, but Black women have faced even greater challenges overcoming prejudice for both their gender *and* their race. Feminist and scholar **ANNA JULIA COOPER** spent her entire career advocating for Black women's education rights, knowing that uplifting Black women in America would uplift the whole nation.

Anna Julia Haywood was born on August 10, 1859, in **Raleigh**, **North Carolina**, to an enslaved mother and enslaver George Washington Haywood. Once the **American Civil War** was over, she attended **Saint Augustine's Normal School and Collegiate Institute** (now Saint Augustine's University), a school for former enslaved people, where she earned a high school-level education. She excelled as a student, and she began teaching math to other pupils at just ten years old. During her time at Saint Augustine's, Anna Julia witnessed her male classmates being encouraged more in the classroom than her fellow female students, which stirred up a lifelong passion for Black women's equality.

She also met her future husband, George A. G. Cooper, at the school. Two years after they married, George passed away. Anna Julia then decided to continue her education and work toward a college degree. She attended **Oberlin College** in **Ohio** on scholarship and earned both a bachelor's and a master's degree in mathematics there. Anna Julia's love for education and learning soon inspired her to find ways to make learning more accessible to other African Americans who were still experiencing discrimination and limited opportunities in the wake of the war. In 1892, she published a book titled *A Voice from the South by a Black Woman of the South*. Her book explained that providing Black women an education would benefit all of American society.

Anna Julia spent the rest of her career working to educate others on the value of Black women's education. She became a notable public speaker, and she also cofounded many civil rights organizations, including the **Colored Women's League**. She also trailblazed her own educational opportunities for most of her life. At the age of sixty-seven, she received a doctorate from the Sorbonne in Paris in 1925. After retiring from teaching in 1930, she became the president of **Frelinghuysen University**—an institution supporting working Black adults in continuing their education.

After almost a century of working toward equality for African American education, Anna Julia passed away on February 27, 1964, at the age of 105 in Washington, DC.

Described by one admirer as a "guerrilla warrior" in the "wilderness of industrial wrongs," social worker and reformer **FLORENCE KELLEY** pursued a life-long crusade to obtain legislation that would improve the terrible working conditions faced by women and children.

Born in Philadelphia, Kelley graduated from **Cornell University** in 1882 with the intention of studying law. Barred from the legal profession in the United States because she was a woman, Kelley did postgraduate work at the **University of Zürich** in Switzerland, the first European university open to women. While abroad, she observed working women in England, learned about reform movements, and translated into English *The Condition of the Working Class in England*, an important book on social reform by the German socialist writer Friedrich Engels.

Kelley returned to the United States, and in 1891, she took up residence in Chicago's **Hull House**, a settlement house run by **Jane Addams** to aid Chicago's poor. Kelley wrote a pamphlet on child labor abuses and investigated sweatshop practices in the garment industry. As a result of her efforts, Illinois passed one of the first factory reform acts to limit hours for women workers, prohibit child labor, and control sweatshops, and Kelley was appointed the state's first chief factory inspector. To help ensure that violators of the new law were prosecuted, she enrolled in evening law school classes at

Northwestern University and earned her law degree in 1894.

In 1899, Kelley moved to New York City's Henry Street Settlement. The same year, she became the head of the **National Consumers League**, an organization dedicated to using consumer pressure through publicity and boycotts to ensure that goods were manufactured and sold under proper working conditions. As head of the League, Kelley also helped create sixty-four local leagues to fight for the same goals on the state and local levels.

Kelley would spend the next thirty years fighting for federal fair labor laws to protect women workers and to eliminate child labor. A lifelong opponent of child labor, Kelley teamed up with **Lillian Wald**, the founder of public health nursing and founder of Henry Street Settlement, and organized the New York Child Labor Committee in 1902; two years later, they helped establish the **National Child Labor Committee**. In 1912, both women were instrumental in the creation of the federal **Children's Bureau**.

In 1909, Kelley began a campaign for minimum wage laws, publishing articles and speaking around the country. Largely thanks to her efforts, by 1913, nine states enacted minimum wage laws.

In addition to her other activities and accomplishments, Kelley was a founder of the **Women's International League for Peace and Freedom**, and for years served as vice president of the **National American Woman Suffrage Association**.

Known as "The Girl of the Western Plains," sharpshooter and Wild West performer **ANNIE OAKLEY** actually grew up east of the Mississippi River in Ohio, north of Cincinnati. Born **Phoebe Ann Moses**, she was placed in an orphanage after her father died, and at the age of ten, she was sent to live with a farm family. However, they overworked and mistreated her, and after two years, she ran away to live with her mother, who had remarried.

A fearless and high-spirited girl, she roamed the woods and fields around her mother's farm on a pony. When she discovered her father's old cap-and-ball rifle, she displayed a natural skill as a sharpshooter. The young girl was soon helping to support her family by shooting game for the Cincinnati market, and as the story goes, she paid off the mortgage on her family's farm with her earnings.

At the age of fifteen, she won a shooting match against professional shooter **Frank Butler**, whom she married in 1876. The couple began touring the country as sharpshooters "Butler and Oakley," the name Annie took, apparently from a Cincinnati suburb.

In 1885, Oakley began performing with **Buffalo Bill's Wild West Show**, where she would star for the next sixteen years, thrilling audiences with her remarkable trick shooting. Taking center stage, Oakley would burst glass balls in midair with her impeccable aim, shoot down targets thrown by cowboy riders with her pistol on horseback, shoot out flames from a revolving wheel of candles while standing on her galloping horse, and riddle a playing card with bullets as it fell. This last trick proved so popular that any often-punched ticket subsequently became known as an "Annie Oakley." The famous American Indian Chief **Sitting Bull**, who joined Buffalo Bill's company in 1885, gave her a Sioux name meaning "**Little Sure Shot**," and regarded her as an adopted daughter.

Oakley toured with Buffalo Bill throughout the United States and Europe. She became a particular favorite with English audiences and met Queen Victoria. In 1901, Annie Oakley's performing career with Buffalo Bill ended when she suffered severe injuries in a Wild West Show train wreck.

After months of convalescence, she was able to return to the stage as a Western heroine in plays and to perform marksmanship feats with her husband. In 1922, a motor accident in Florida left her partially paralyzed, and she returned to her native Ohio. She died there four years later at the age of sixty-six. For several generations of Americans, Annie Oakley was the embodiment of the skilled western frontierswoman.

When **JULIETTE GORDON LOW** founded the **Girl Scouts of the USA** in 1912, she believed that intellectual, physical, and moral strength were as important to the development of girls as the learning of skills that would make them good homemakers, wives, and mothers. Low's niece, **Daisy Gordon**, was registered as the first Girl Scout in America, and the first troop consisted of eighteen girls. By 1927, the year of Low's death, Girl Scout membership numbered nearly one hundred sixty-eight thousand, and by the end of the twentieth century, it had reached 3.5 million, becoming the largest voluntary organization for girls and young women in the world.

Juliette Gordon was born into a wealthy and distinguished family in Savannah, Georgia, and received an excellent private school education. On a trip to England, she met **William Low**, the son of a wealthy cotton merchant, and they married in 1886. After his death in 1905, she began to travel extensively in search of direction for her life. In 1911, while in England, Low met British military hero Sir **Robert Baden-Powell** and his sister **Agnes**, who had founded the Boy Scouts and the Girl Guides. Inspired by the Baden-Powells' work in scouting, Low formed her own Girl Guides troops in Scotland and London and returned to Savannah with a determined mind to bring the Girl Guide movement to the United States.

Originally outfitted in dark blue middy blouses, skirts, and a light blue tie, Low's early Girl Guides—who would become the Girl Scouts in 1913—pursued badges in diverse areas like telegraphy, farming, and electrical work. In addition, the Girl Scout handbook contained practical advice on various topics, such as "How to kill and dress poultry" and "How to secure a burglar with six inches of cord," as well as articles on radical subjects including ecology, organic foods, and career opportunities for women. Low paid for the expenses of the organization out of her own pocket until 1917, while she crisscrossed the country to recruit prominent women to take up roles as leaders and sponsors of Girl Scout troops.

During World War I, the Girl Scouts volunteered their services by working in hospitals, staffing railroad station canteens for trains transporting soldiers, growing vegetables, and selling war bonds. Under Low's leadership, their record of service established the Girl Scouts as a national organization, which resulted in a significant expansion of membership. Low resigned as president in 1920 but continued her organizational activities up to her death from cancer in 1927.

The millions of American girls who benefited from their involvement in the Girl Scouts owe a debt of gratitude to Juliette Gordon Low, a woman with a vision that girls should pursue an active life and achieve their full potential.

CHARLOTTE PERKINS GILMAN is acknowledged as one the first and most important writers to describe the difficulties that women faced in the late nineteenth and early twentieth centuries because of the assumptions American society made about their roles as wives and mothers.

Charlotte Gilman was born in Hartford, Connecticut, to Mary and Frederic Beecher Perkins. Her father was the nephew of **Harriet Beecher Stowe**, the author of *Uncle Tom's Cabin*. As a young woman, Charlotte worked as an art teacher, governess, and commercial artist, designing greeting cards and writing poetry.

In 1884, she married fellow artist, **Charles Walter Stetson**, and a year later gave birth to their daughter, Katherine. Shortly after, she began battling bouts of severe depression, a condition that would be identified today as **postpartum depression**. She eventually sought treatment from an eminent nerve specialist, who prescribed a cure of complete bed rest in total isolation. She was not allowed to read, write, talk to others, or even feed herself.

"I went home," Gilman later recalled, "followed those directions rigidly for months, and came perilously near to losing my mind." She eventually abandoned the rest cure and took control of her own recovery.

Gilman separated from her husband in 1888, and they divorced in 1894. When he remarried a close friend of hers, she granted the couple custody of her daughter.

In 1892, Gilman published her short story, "The Yellow Wallpaper," in *New England Magazine*. A feminist classic, the story concerns the difficulties and subsequent breakdown of a woman artist torn between her desire to write and the expectations placed on her as a wife and mother.

In 1898, Gilman published *Women and Economics*, an analysis of the fate of women in America's male-oriented, capitalist society. Hailed as one of the key theoretical texts of the early women's movement, the book examines the "sexuo-economic" relationship between men and women.

Gilman claimed that society expected women to accentuate their feminine characteristics in order to attract and please men. This, in turn, led to economic dependence on men and caused a great detriment to women as individuals as well as being harmful to society overall. Translated into several languages, the book brought Gilman international renown.

Over the next thirty-five years, Gilman continued to write fiction and nonfiction stories, articles, and books advocating economic, political, and social independence for women. In her early forties, she married again—this time happily to a cousin, George Houghton Gilman. She continued to work throughout the marriage, and eventually her daughter returned to live with her.

In 1932, Gilman was diagnosed with breast cancer. Three years later, when the illness began seriously affecting her daily life, she died by suicide.

An American novelist who shone a realistic and unfiltered light on society's **Gilded Age**, **EDITH WHARTON** built a successful writing career spanning several decades at a time when women were expected to do little more than get married and raise children. She became the first woman to be awarded a **Pulitzer Prize** for her iconic novel *The Age of Innocence.*

Edith Wharton was born in 1862 to a prominent and wealthy **New York** family. She spent a lot of time living in Europe at a young age, splitting her time between France, Italy, and Germany just after the **American Civil War**. From early childhood, Edith grew up to be a passionate reader, and her time in Europe inspired a deep appreciation for language and literature. She returned to New York high society for her teenage years and resumed her studies until she officially entered the social scene. At sixteen years old, she privately published her first work—*Verses*, a volume of poems.

In 1885, at the age of twenty-three, she married Boston banker Edward Wharton. Several years into their marriage, Wharton began her writing career. She coauthored *The Decoration of Houses*, which showcased her knowledge of design and architecture, and she contributed short pieces to magazines. Wharton gained widespread attention for her novel *The House of Mirth*, published in 1905, which criticized the high society in which she was raised.

In 1913, Wharton divorced her husband and moved to France permanently. When **World War I** broke out in Europe, instead of escaping to safer locations in England or the United States, she remained in Paris and contributed to the war efforts there. She arranged for workrooms, lodging, and schools for those who were impacted by the war. She dedicated her time and risked her safety to report on the front lines as one of very few journalists or writers who were allowed.

Wharton published *The Age of Innocence* in 1920, and the novel showcased the social pressures of high society. It won her the 1921 Pulitzer Prize for Fiction, making her the first woman to win the award in history.

Over her lifetime, Wharton wrote fifty books and contributed countless articles and short stories to other publications. She found commercial and critical success writing across a wide range of genres and about varied topics at a time when many female authors were not taken as seriously as male authors. Wharton died in France at the age of seventy-five on August 11, 1937. Her popular works of fiction have lived on long past her death, captivating readers with her beautiful writing and brave critiques of her own society.

Considered to be the "first woman geologist in America," **FLORENCE BASCOM** is known not only for her pioneering work in her field but also for the gender barriers she broke professionally.

Born in 1862 in Williamstown, Massachusetts, Florence Bascom was raised in a family that was considered progressive for the time. Her father, John Bascom, was a professor at Williams College, and her mother, Emma Curtiss Bascom, was an activist and educator who was involved in the fight for women's suffrage. Florence's parents believed strongly in equal rights for women and **coeducation**. Her father often took Florence and her siblings on trips into the mountains and wilderness, which fostered Florence's interest in science from an early age.

When Bascom's father took up the post of president at the University of Wisconsin in 1874, the family moved to Wisconsin. The university began accepting women in 1875, and two years later, Florence enrolled. However, even though the university allowed women to enroll, Florence and other female students still faced adversity because of their gender. They weren't allowed in classrooms that were already filled with male students, and their access to the library and other facilities was limited. Despite these obstacles, Bascom completed two bachelor's degrees there—the first in arts and letters in 1882 and the second in science in 1884—and a master's degree in geology in 1887. Determined to also complete a PhD, Bascom soon enrolled at Johns Hopkins University. The school had only recently started admitting female students, and Bascom was forced to sit hidden behind a screen during her classes, so that she wouldn't "distract" her male classmates. Despite this discrimination, Bascom received her **PhD in geology** in 1893, making her the second woman in the United States ever to earn a doctorate in that field.

After earning her degrees, Bascom began teaching at Ohio State University before moving to Bryn Mawr College, where she founded the department for geology and started an extensive collection of rocks, minerals, and fossils.

In 1896, Bascom became the first woman to work for the **United States Geological Survey (USGS)**, the government agency that studies the country's landscape and natural resources. She was assigned to study a section of the Mid-Atlantic **Piedmont region** plateau. Bascom spent her summers mapping the different types of rocks in the region and studied thin sections of the rocks that she collected as samples. She focused on the intricate layering in the rocks she collected and wrote articles about her research, which helped scientists understand how mountains are formed. She also made observations that contributed to the scientific understanding of erosion cycles in the region.

Bascom served as an associate editor of the *American Geologist* from 1896 to 1908. She was as member of the National Academy of Sciences and the National Research Council. In 1924 she was elected to the Council of the **Geological Society of America**, and in 1930, she became the vice president of the society—the first woman to serve in either role.

The most famed journalist of her day, and the first woman investigative reporter, **NELLIE BLY** was born **Elizabeth Cochran** in a small town near Pittsburgh, Pennsylvania. With only one year of formal education, she got her start in journalism at nineteen by responding to a *Pittsburgh Dispatch* newspaper editorial titled "What Girls Are Good For." The column strongly opposed the idea of women's suffrage and careers for women. Her angry reply in support of women's rights so impressed the editor that he asked her to come in for an interview—and then hired her.

Concerned about family disapproval of her new career, she used a byline of "Nellie Bly" after a popular Stephen Foster song. Rather than write the traditional "feminine" articles that her new editor expected, Bly investigated and reported on subjects such as hazardous and exploitative working conditions facing women in factories and destitution in the slums of the city's poorest citizens.

In 1887, Bly gained a job with Joseph Pulitzer's *New York World* newspaper and won national notoriety by reporting on the brutality and neglect endured by patients in mental hospitals. To get her story, Bly feigned insanity to get confined for treatment at New York City's notorious asylum on **Blackwell's Island**. After Pulitzer secured her release, she wrote a chilling account of what she saw and experienced, prompting a public investigation and much-needed reforms.

Bly subsequently went undercover as a sweatshop worker to report on the appalling working conditions that women endured in the garment industry. She also got herself arrested for theft in order to reveal the indignities faced by women prisoners in city jails. Her first-hand accounts of these abuses soon earned Bly the reputation as **"the best reporter in America."**

Her most famous adventure took place in November 1889, when she set out to break the round-the-world record "set" by Jules Verne's fictional hero Phileas Fogg in *Around the World in Eighty Days*. Crossing the Atlantic and the Mediterranean by ship and traveling throughout the Middle East and Asia by train, rickshaw, and sampan, her adventures were followed daily in newspapers around the world. Bly returned to New York to a parade after a seventy-two-day, six-hour, and eleven-minute journey.

In 1895, Bly married seventy-two-year-old **Robert L. Seaman**, a man she had only known briefly. The lived quietly together for fifteen years, and after he died in 1910, she tried unsuccessfully to continue his manufacturing business. After living abroad for a time, she returned to New York and spent her final years as a reporter for the *New York Journal*.

Noted as the first African American woman to charter a bank in the United States, businesswoman **MAGGIE L. WALKER** pushed for lasting improvements in opportunity and quality of life for African Americans and women in post–Civil War America. Her focus on improvement, integrity, and success in business reframed possibility for her African American community.

Maggie Lena Draper was born in **Richmond, Virginia**, in July 1864, just two years after the end of the American Civil War. Her mother was a formerly enslaved woman, and her biological father was Eccles Cuthbert, a Confederate soldier. Her mother married William Mitchell, and Maggie took her stepfather's last name. After her stepfather passed away unexpectedly in 1876, her single mother singlehandedly supported her family as a laundry worker. Maggie often assisted her mother and delivered clothes to customers around town.

When she was a young teenager, Maggie joined the Grand Order of St. Luke (later renamed Independent Order of St. Luke)—a local society that provided support for African Americans in the community. The group worked to improve feelings of integrity and connectedness within the African American community in the wake of the **American Civil War**.

After graduating from school, Maggie taught grade school students for a few years before marrying Armstead Walker Jr. After marrying, Maggie quit her teaching job to focus on raising her family. At this time, she also increased her involvement with the Order, where her responsibilities grew considerably as the years passed. In 1899, she was appointed executive secretary-treasurer, a top leadership position. With her guidance and resolve, the organization grew considerably all around the nation and its financial state improved greatly. Maggie became known as a focused businesswomen with great instincts and sound decision-making.

In 1902, Maggie established the *St. Luke Herald*—a newspaper intended to improve communications between the Order and the community. The next year, she then established the St. Luke Penny Savings Bank, making her the first African American woman to charter a bank in U.S. history.

She was also heavily involved in civil rights organizations. She served in leadership positions for the **National Association of Colored Women (NACW)**, the **National Association for the Advancement of Colored People (NAACP)**, and the **Virginia Interracial Commission**, among others. She was committed to finding ways to improve the quality of life and opportunity for African Americans.

In 1915, Maggie's husband died unexpectedly, but due to her business acumen and success, she was able to comfortably support her family alone. She was even able to add onto her family home to provide space for her sons' growing families and her mother later in life.

Maggie continued to work and lead the bank and the Order late into her life. Even as her health declined and required her to use a wheelchair in the late 1920s, she continued to push forward. Maggie L. Walker passed away on December 15, 1934, at the age of seventy.

LYDA CONLEY was the first **American Indian** woman to argue a case in front of the **U.S. Supreme Court**. Throughout her life, she relentlessly pursued knowledge, education, and a platform to protect her ancestry and uphold her culture's traditions and rights.

Lyda Conley was born in 1869 to Elizabeth Burton Zane, a member of the **Wyandot Nation**, and Andrew Syrenus Conley, a European American. She was raised on a farm in **Kansas**, and she faced immeasurable challenges at a young age. Conley's mother and one of her sisters died during her childhood, followed soon by her father and grandmother. All her deceased relatives were buried in the Wyandot National Burying Ground in **Kansas City**. Conley and two of her sisters looked after themselves for the rest of their adolescence, and they lived in poverty through most of it.

By the mid-1880s, Kansas City, and specifically the location of the burial ground, became highly sought-after real estate. Conley felt responsible for protecting the Wyandot's sacred land and history, so she enrolled in law school. She graduated from the Kansas City School of Law in 1902, and she became the first woman admitted to the Kansas Bar Association.

In 1906, when attempts were made to change legislation and excavate the bodies there, Conley and her sisters relocated to the cemetery and armed themselves to protect their ancestors and relatives buried there. They built a makeshift fort and stood watch over the land, ensuring no one would disturb the graves. She was quoted in the *Kansas City Times* saying, "Why should we not be proud of our ancestors and protect their graves? We shall do it, and woe be to the man that first attempts to steal a body. We are part owners of the ground and have the right under the law to keep off trespassers, the right a man has to shoot a burglar who enters his home."

Conley prepared a petition arguing the land sale was unconstitutional, pointing toward a treaty from 1855. Her local court ruled against her, but she appealed her case until it reached the U.S. Supreme Court, where the case was heard.

In 1909, Conley became the first American Indian woman admitted to argue a case in front of the U.S. Supreme Court. The court eventually ruled against her, but that did not strip Conley of her accomplishment. The sisters continued to protect the burial ground nonetheless, and their persistence spurred attention. Their efforts would not be in vain; a Kansas senator, Charles Curtis, who was part American Indian, sympathized with their struggle and worked to pass a law protecting the cemetery from any attempts to build.

Lyda Conley died on May 28, 1946, and she was buried in the ground that she spent her life protecting. Although laws were passed to protect the land, many attempts were made over many years to release rights to the land. In 2017, officials declared the location a **National Historic Landmark (NHL)**, protecting it from further interference.

EMMA GOLDMAN stirred up more controversy than any other social or **political activist** of the early twentieth century. Her critics condemned her for her campaigns on behalf of free speech, individual liberty, and women's rights, and the American government eventually deported her for her activism.

Born in the Jewish ghetto of Kovno, Russia, Goldman immigrated to Rochester, New York, in 1885 to escape an arranged marriage. She went to work in a clothing sweatshop, where she earned $2.50 a week and was shocked by the terrible treatment of the workers. The experience made her distrust the capitalist system, and she became an activist in the **anarchist movement**, which promoted social equality without government interference.

In 1889, Goldman moved to New York City, where she met **Alexander Berkman**, a Russian American anarchist who became her longtime partner. In 1893, she was sentenced to a one-year prison term for inciting a riot among a group of unemployed workers in New York's Union Square. In prison, Goldman studied nursing, and after her release, she studied midwifery and nursing in Vienna for a year.

During the first years of the twentieth century, Goldman renounced calls for violence, even though figures like **Leon Czolgosz**, who assassinated President McKinley in 1901, claimed to have been inspired by her activities. For the next several years, Goldman traveled around the United States lecturing on anarchism, social equality and justice, and workers' and women's rights. She was also one of the first people to speak out publicly about women's reproductive rights, and she greatly influenced **Margaret Sanger**, who is credited with founding the birth control movement in the United States.

In 1917, Goldman was sentenced to two years in a federal prison for speaking out against the draft during World War I. Upon her release, the American government repatriated her to Russia. There, despite her socialist and communist sympathies, she became an outspoken critic of the Bolsheviks' suppression of civil liberties after they transformed Russia into the Soviet Union.

In 1921, Goldman went to Sweden and then Germany, where she condemned totalitarianism in newspaper articles and in her book *My Disillusionment in Russia* (1923). In 1931, she published her autobiography *Living My Life*.

During the **Spanish Civil War** (1936–1939), Goldman worked tirelessly for the doomed Republican cause against the fascist forces led by General Francisco Franco. In 1940, after she suffered a fatal stroke, the American government allowed her body to be returned home for burial in a Chicago cemetery.

Emma Goldman had a lifelong uncompromising commitment to social equality and justice. Despite her controversial activities, as one historian stated, she "had lived to the end a life of unique integrity."

Although she didn't officially begin her career until her mid-fifties, **YNES MEXIA'S** passion for nature and the environment led to not only her designation as the first Mexican American female botanist in the field, but also one of the most successful and influential botanists in history. She was a champion for conservationism, faced adversity for being both a woman and a Mexican American in a scientific field dominated by white men, and proved to be an example for others hoping to pursue a passion late into their lives.

Ynes Mexia was born in Washington, DC, on May 24, 1870. She was a very shy child who endured a challenging childhood, but she often used the world of reading and the great outdoors as safe spaces to explore, play, and find joy. After finishing school, Mexia relocated to **Mexico** to assist her father on a family ranch. She spent three decades there, marrying twice and ending her second marriage in divorce.

It wasn't until Mexia moved to **San Francisco** in 1909 to seek help for her mental health challenges that she realized she had a passion for environmentalism and conservation. At first, Mexia intended to study sociology and start a new life after two failed marriages by her late thirties. However, in her free time, she joined the **Northern California Sierra Club**—an organization promoting environmental conservation in the **American Pacific Northwest**—as well as the **Save the Redwoods League**—an organization with the mission of saving the famous redwood trees in northern California. What started as a fulfilling hobby for Mexia soon turned into a new life mission.

At fifty-one, Mexia decided to go back to school and study botany at the University of California, Berkeley. In 1925, Mexia ventured to Mexico on her first collection trip for plants through a group study at Stanford University. In this setting, Mexia realized she disliked group botany work, and she soon broke off from her group, staying in Mexico for two years. While there, she collected thousands of specimens, including the first of many plants to be named after her—the *Mimosa Mexiae*. She moved on from Mexico to **South America**, putting herself in incredibly dangerous environments—including the **Amazon Rainforest**—in order to collect plants.

Mexia traveled the Americas for over a decade, collecting and researching independently at a time when world travel and botany work were performed by men. On her travels, she was often confronted by locals or fellow travelers who thought her passion and choices were inappropriate, but she relished in their judgments, continuing on her journey. Mexia worked in her field relentlessly right up until her passing on July 12, 1938, at the age of sixty-eight, illustrating that anyone can explore a passion and find a new life purpose at any age. Her career was just thirteen years long, but she became known as one of the most influential botanists in history.

A physician and a medical researcher, **FLORENCE RENA SABIN** was one of the most influential American women scientists of her time. Her study of the lymphatic system made it possible to understand the origin of blood cells and blood vessels, and her research on tuberculosis led to better treatment of the widespread, often-fatal disease.

Florence Rena Sabin was born in the mining town of Central City, Colorado, the younger daughter of a mining engineer. Her mother, a teacher, died when Florence was four, and after attending boarding schools in Denver and Illinois, she was sent at the age of twelve to live with her grandparents in Vermont. She attended **Vermont Academy** and **Smith College**, where she graduated with a Bachelor of Science degree in 1893. She went on to study medicine at **Johns Hopkins University**, and while she was a student there, she constructed accurate models of the brain that were later used as teaching aids in several medical schools.

During her college years, Sabin was active in the Baltimore **women's suffrage movement**, sometimes speaking in public for the cause. In 1900, she became the first woman to receive a medical degree from Johns Hopkins. She interned at Johns Hopkins Hospital and then turned to teaching and research of the lymphatic system.

In 1917, Sabin became the first woman at Johns Hopkins to attain the position of full professor.

From 1924 to 1926, Sabin served as president of the **American Association of Anatomists**, and in 1925, she became the first woman elected to the prestigious **National Academy of Science**. That same year she accepted a position at New York City's **Rockefeller Institute** (later Rockefeller University), an association dedicated to scientific research. The first woman member of the institute, Sabin directed a team of researchers in groundbreaking work on the biological causes of tuberculosis.

Sabin retired from the Rockefeller Institute in 1938 and returned to Colorado, where the governor appointed her chair of a state subcommittee on public health. As a result of Sabin's work, Colorado passed the **Sabin Health Bills**, which led to a massive drop in the death rate from tuberculosis.

At the age of seventy-six, Sabin was appointed manager of Denver's Department of Health and Welfare. She served in that position for five years and then retired to care for her ailing sister. She died of a heart attack in Denver in October 1953. A bronze statue of Florence Rena Sabin, shown sitting at her microscope, can now be found in the **Statuary Hall** in the U.S. Capitol building in Washington, DC.

A prolific writer and patron of the arts, **GERTRUDE STEIN** encouraged and influenced some of the most important writers and artists of the twentieth century. Stein also wrote nearly six hundred works of her own—experimental plays, poems, novels, biographies, essays, and opera librettos—in which she used language in ways that contributed to new forms of modern literature.

Born in Allegheny, Pennsylvania, Stein was the youngest of seven children. She grew up in Oakland, California, where her father made a fortune investing in real estate. She studied philosophy and psychology at the Harvard Annex, which later became Radcliffe College, in Cambridge, Massachusetts.

After graduating from Radcliffe in 1897, Stein briefly studied medicine at Johns Hopkins University Medical School. In 1903, after a year in Italy, London, and back in America, she settled in Paris. At first, she shared an apartment with her brother Leo and then later with **Alice B. Toklas**, whom she met around this time and who would become her life partner.

Stein's address at **27 rue de Fleurus** became famous, especially during the 1920s for the now well-known abstract painters and modern writers who had flocked to the salons she hosted. One of these artists, **Pablo Picasso**, painted a famous portrait of Stein. The writers who visited Stein's apartment included soon-to-be literary giants like **F. Scott Fitzgerald**, **James Joyce**, and **Ernest Hemingway**.

In her own writing, Stein was more interested in the sound of words than in their meaning, and she tried to capture the spirit of abstract painting. Her work was both criticized for being unreadable and praised for her unique style of writing, which often involved the use of repetition and rhythm, as in the often-quoted phrase, "A rose is a rose is a rose is a rose."

Some of Stein's noted works are her thousand-page novel, *The Making of Americans, or The History of a Family's Progress* (1925), *Operas and Plays* (1932), and *Lectures in America* (1935). Her most famous work is *The Autobiography of Alice B. Toklas* (1933), which is really Stein's own autobiography written from Toklas's point of view. Several of Stein's works were published years after they were completed or posthumously.

In 1937, Stein and Toklas moved to a new apartment in Paris, where they remained until the outbreak of World War II. After German forces occupied France in 1940, the couple moved to their country home in the small town of Culoz. They returned to Paris following the city's liberation by American troops in 1944 and were visited by many soldiers eager to meet and talk with the legendary Gertrude Stein.

Gertrude Stein died of cancer in 1946 and was buried in Paris.

◆ A founding member of the **Society of American Indians**, **LAURA CORNELIUS KELLOGG** was a powerful, relentless voice who advocated for **American Indian rights** in the early twentieth century. She used her superior writing and oratory skills to inspire other American Indians to stay firm in their identities as the nation progressed into the **modern era**.

Kellogg was born on an **Oneida Indian Reservation** in **Green Bay, Wisconsin**, on September 10, 1880. She was born into a well-known and powerful family of tribal leaders, which provided her with a strong pride in her heritage.

In her youth, Kellogg attended an Episcopal boarding school in Fond du Lac, Wisconsin, when many of her tribal peers attended Indian-specific boarding schools much farther away. In her twenties, she took courses at many respected schools, such as Cornell University and Stanford University. Kellogg became an expert at her native Oneida language as well as Mohawk and English; soon, she was considered a captivating public speaker by audiences of all backgrounds.

In her speaking and writing, Kellogg was passionate about tribal rights and discussing her opposition to legislation that had moved her people off their original land in **New York** in the early 1820s. She was firm in protecting the identities of the Wisconsin Oneida at a time when there were strong pressures to Americanize. In 1911,

Kellogg was one founding member of the Society of American Indians, a group dedicated to improving quality of life and opportunity for Native Americans. She contributed to the group for a short time, but she left the organization once it became clear that she strongly opposed the society's direction, which considered embracing the new circumstances. Kellogg wanted American Indians to remain autonomous from the American government while being self-sufficient and retaining their identities without outside cultural interference.

Laura then shifted her attention to raising awareness and funds to fight for native rights to indigenous lands that were taken from them. She and her husband encouraged support around the United States and Canada for legal efforts. In the end, courts dismissed their lawsuit. Officials also criticized the pair for their questionable fundraising, but they were never prosecuted.

Even after the failed lawsuit attempts, Kellogg continued to fight for the independence of native tribes, but she lost a lot of support and interest once **President Franklin D. Roosevelt** introduced the **New Deal**, which included attractive incentives for indigenous cultures.

Although Kellogg's support fizzled out toward the end of her life, she is seen by some as an incredible example for a new generation of native people fighting for their land and identity rights.

JEANETTE RANKIN was the first woman elected to the U.S. Congress. A strong suffragist, she also helped women gain the vote in her native state of Montana five years before the Nineteenth Amendment granted universal suffrage to women throughout the country.

Born near Missoula in Montana Territory (now the state of Montana), Rankin was the oldest of seven children. Her father was a successful rancher and lumber merchant, and her mother had been a schoolteacher before her marriage. Rankin was educated at public schools in Missoula, and in 1902, she graduated with a bachelor of science degree from the University of Montana.

In 1908, Rankin went to New York to study at the **New York School of Philanthropy**. She briefly practiced social work in Montana and Washington and then entered the University of Washington.

Beginning in 1910, she became active in the **suffragist movement**. She urged the Montana State Legislature to give women the vote, served as field secretary for the **National American Woman Suffrage Association (NAWSA)**, and lobbied for suffrage in fifteen states. In 1914, her efforts paid off when her home state granted women the right to vote.

In 1916, Rankin ran for Congress as a Republican and made history when she was elected the **first woman to hold a seat in the U.S. House of Representatives**. In April 1917, Rankin, a pacifist and member of the **Woman's Peace Party (WPP)**, voted against America's entry into World War I. She was denounced for her vote by the press, the church, and suffragists such as NAWSA president **Carrie Chapman Catt**, who believed that women should support the war effort. Rankin spent the rest of her term sponsoring protective legislation for children and continued to work for passage of a federal suffrage amendment.

After making an unsuccessful attempt to become Montana's first woman senator, Rankin returned to private life in 1919. She spent the next twenty years working on behalf of numerous national and international peace organizations, as well as continuing to push for the passage of legislation designed to benefit women and children.

In 1940, she won reelection to Congress, running as a Republican pacifist. On December 8, 1941, the day after the Japanese attacked Pearl Harbor, Rankin cast the only vote against America's entry into World War II. Because of her vote, Rankin lost her chances for reelection.

In the late 1960s, Rankin again made news as she led the **Jeanette Rankin Brigade**, a group of feminists, pacifists, students, and other activists opposed to the Vietnam War. Well into her eighties, she demonstrated with the group in Washington, DC, in January 1968. Shortly afterward, Rankin decided to run for Congress again, but failing health prevented her from beginning a campaign.

Jeanette Rankin died in California at the age of ninety-two.

ROSE SCHNEIDERMAN fought for women workers' right to join labor unions. An influential labor leader, she helped to better the lives of women forced to work long hours for low pay in hazardous sweatshop conditions.

Born in a shtetl (Jewish village) called Sawin in Russian Poland (now Poland), Schneiderman was the eldest of four children. Her father was a tailor and her mother a seamstress.

The Schneidermans immigrated to the United States in 1890, and the family settled in a two-room tenement apartment on the Lower East Side of New York City. Rose attended school there off and on, and she eventually received the equivalent of a ninth-grade education.

At the age of thirteen, she began her first job as a cashier and clerk in a department store, at times working a seventy-hour week for a salary of $2.75. In 1898, she took a slightly better paying position as a lining-maker in a cap factory. The wages were still low, however, and employees were responsible for buying their own sewing machines and replacing machines that broke down.

Schneiderman began her career as a **labor union activist** in 1903, when she and two other women employees organized the first all-women Local 23 of the **Jewish Socialist United Cloth Hat and Cap Makers' Union**. The following year, Schneiderman became the first woman to hold a national office in an American labor union, when she was elected to the union's **General Executive Board**.

In 1905, she led the union in a thirteen-week strike against her employers' attempts to institute an open shop policy—hiring lower-paid workers from outside the union. Schneiderman also played a key role in organizing the massive garment workers strike of 1909–1910.

Beginning in 1905, Schneiderman worked closely with the **Women's Trade Union League** (**WTUL**) and the **International Ladies Garment Workers Union** (**ILGWU**), organizing local unions and leading strikes. She was president of the New York branch of the WTUL from 1918–1949, and in 1926, she was elected president of the national WTUL.

During the 1920s, Schneiderman lobbied for protective legislation, such as minimum wage and eight-hour workday laws for women workers. Partly due to her efforts, such legislation was enacted in New York during the 1930s.

In 1933, President Franklin D. Roosevelt appointed Schneiderman to the labor advisory board of the **National Recovery Administration**. The only woman on the board, her job was to ensure that industries employing women followed codes regulating wages and hours. From 1937 to 1943, Schneiderman served as secretary of the **New York State Department of Labor**.

Schneiderman retired from public life after the WTUL closed its branches in 1955. In 1967, she published her autobiography titled *All for One*. She died in 1972 at the age of ninety.

ALICE PAUL helped lead the final push for a constitutional amendment guaranteeing women the right to vote. Unlike **Carrie Chapman Catt**, Paul took a much more militant approach in obtaining the vote for women—including organizing massive street demonstrations which led to her arrest and imprisonment on several occasions.

Born in Mount Laurel, New Jersey, Alice Paul was the eldest of four children in a well-to-do Quaker family. Her mother was a suffragist, and one of Paul's earliest memories was of accompanying her mother to a suffrage meeting. Paul attended Quaker schools and **Swarthmore College**, graduating with a degree in biology in 1905. She studied at the **New York School of Philanthropy** and went on to earn a master's degree and a PhD in sociology from the University of Pennsylvania.

In 1907, Paul went to England, where she became involved in the **British suffrage movement**. She joined suffragettes in their demonstrations, was repeatedly arrested, and participated in prison hunger strikes. After returning to the United States in 1910, she continued to fight for women suffrage, serving as chair of the congressional committee of the **NAWSA**.

However, Paul and several other committee members disagreed on strategy with NAWSA president Carrie Chapman Catt. In 1913, they formed their own group, the **Congressional Union for Women Suffrage**, and adopted more defiant tactics than NAWSA to obtain their goal.

On March 3, 1913, the eve of Woodrow Wilson's presidential inauguration, Paul led more than five thousand women in a march in Washington, DC, to press for adoption of a women's suffrage amendment. The demonstration provoked violent reactions from crowds of male onlookers; many women were hospitalized, and armed troops had to restore order. The hostility that greeted the demonstrators caused an outpouring of national sympathy for the cause.

In 1916, Paul helped form the **National Women's Party** to work for passage of the Nineteenth Amendment, which was finally ratified in 1920. Paul then began a crusade for the **Equal Rights Amendment (ERA)**, which she authored in 1923 and then introduced to Congress that same year. Paul also headed the **Women's Research Foundation** from 1927 to 1937, and in the 1930s, she helped found the World's Woman's Party. In the 1940s, she was instrumental in seeing that the United Nations Charter included references to gender equality.

Alice Paul campaigned for passage of the ERA for nearly fifty years. In 1972, the amendment passed Congress and went to the states for ratification. By 1977, the year of Paul's death, the amendment needed only three more states for adoption. However, it ultimately failed ratification by the 1982 deadline, and died.

JOVITA IDÁR was a fearless journalist and activist who risked her safety and future to inspire fellow **Mexican Americans** to reach for opportunity in the face of rampant discrimination in the **American Southwest**. She spent her life working to preserve and protect Mexican heritage and community and **women's rights** when American society was working to extinguish it.

Idár was born in **Laredo**, **Texas**, on September 7, 1885. She was one of eight children and enjoyed a relatively privileged

upbringing as a Mexican American girl, being provided quality education from a young age. Idár learned about activism in her childhood because her father was a journalist and advocate.

After attending school and working briefly as a teacher, Idár left her job to work at her father's newspaper, *La Crónica*. Jovita had witnessed discrimination and segregation of Mexican American students, and she was also appalled by recent Mexican American lynchings in her area. She saw working at the paper as a way to fight against the discrimination.

Her family used the newspaper to expose injustices Mexican Americans were facing in Texas and support the **Mexican Revolution**, which was occurring just south of the border at the time.

Idár soon moved into writing specifically for women. She started writing articles to advocate for women's equality, and she started to gain attention for her poise and activism. In October 1911, she founded La Liga Femenil Mexicanista, an activist organization specifically for women to fight for change. The organization's first challenge was improving educational opportunities for Mexican American students in their area.

Later, after volunteering in Mexico as a nurse during the war, Idár started working at a new newspaper, where she wrote an outspoken article criticizing **President Woodrow Wilson** and his decision to engage the army at the U.S.–Mexico border. The president sent **Texas Rangers** to the newspaper office to confront and intimidate Idár for her criticism. Idár stood firm and brave and did not let the Rangers into the offices; she reminded them that her work was protected under the **First Amendment of the U.S. Constitution**. The men retreated, but they later returned and destroyed the newspaper offices.

Although law enforcement used its power to silence the newspaper, Idár continued to use her own voice to fight for Mexican American rights. She returned to her family newspaper, taking it over after her father's death. Later in life, she moved to San Antonio, Texas, where she worked within the **Democratic Party** as a precinct judge. Before her death at sixty in June 1946, Idár continued to work toward equality and improving lives of women and children.

A pioneering composer at a time when there was no path for African American females in the industry, **FLORENCE PRICE** was the first African American woman to have her work performed by a major orchestra. She fought hard to find commercial success for her work, knowing she deserved to earn a living for her gifts just as others did. Today, her work is considered revolutionary, but she did not receive such notoriety until after her death.

Price was born on April 9, 1887, in **Little Rock, Arkansas**. Her father was a dentist—one of very few African American dentists in America at the time—and her mother had worked as an elementary music teacher. Although circumstances were difficult for African Americans living in the **American South** at the time, Price received a stellar music education starting at a young age. She started learning music very young from her mother, and she performed her first piano recital at four years old. Her studies progressed quickly, and she graduated from high school at the age of fourteen as valedictorian before moving on to study at the **New England Conservatory of Music**; she graduated from there in 1906.

Price taught at a local school and also provided private music lessons before joining the staff at Clark University (now Clark Atlanta University) in Atlanta, Georgia. A few years later, she returned to Little Rock and got married to a young lawyer, continued to teach music to private students, and had three children.

In the late 1920s, Price separated from her husband and moved to **Chicago, Illinois**, to escape the oppression and violence African Americans were facing in the South. In Chicago, she found success selling her compositions to publishers who produced sheet music for beginner musicians. She continued teaching in the community, and she found some opportunities to write music for commercials.

The music community started to notice Price's talent. In 1932, her **Symphony in E Minor** was selected for first place in the Rodman Wanamaker Contest in Musical Composition, a prestigious competition for African American composers who were often shut out of the white-dominated industry.

Price premiered her piece at the **1933 Chicago World's Fair**—also known as the Century of Progress International Exposition. This performance was the first time in U.S. history that a major orchestra performed a symphony written by an African American woman. Throughout the thirties, Price carved out a space for herself in Chicago's music community, and her work earned even more exposure when **Marian Anderson**, a renowned opera singer and groundbreaking African American artist in her own right, performed her work.

For the rest of her life, Price continued to pursue acknowledgment for her work on a wider scale. She knew she had a right to be considered a peer alongside well-known composers who did not face the same challenges that women and African Americans faced while pursuing their dreams. Price passed away on June 3, 1953.

One of America's most renowned and influential artists, **GEORGIA O'KEEFFE** was famous for the unique way in which she used light, color, and space in her paintings.

O'Keeffe was born in Sun Prairie, Wisconsin, the second of seven children. Gifted in art as a child, she later said that she knew by the age of ten that she would be an artist. She attended a convent school in Madison, Wisconsin, until 1902, when her family moved to Williamsburg, Virginia. There, O'Keeffe continued her education at Chatham, a girl's boarding school, where she was awarded a special art diploma upon graduation. She went on to study art at the **Art Institute of Chicago** and the **Art Students' League** in New York, supporting herself by working as an advertising illustrator and a teacher.

In 1915, a friend showed O'Keeffe's drawings to **Alfred Stieglitz**, a well-known photographer and an important figure in the New York art world. He exhibited the drawings at his famous 291 Gallery, and in 1917, he sponsored the first of twenty one-woman shows for O'Keeffe. In 1924, Stieglitz and O'Keeffe married.

O'Keeffe became the only woman in a group of modern artists known as the **Stieglitz Circle**. She was also the subject of some five hundred photographs Stieglitz took of her from 1917 to 1937. During the 1920s, O'Keeffe began to paint abstract and magnified representations of flowers, city scenes, and farmhouses. Her "blown-up" images of flowers, such as **Black Iris** (1926) are favorites with many admirers.

Beginning in 1929, O'Keeffe began spending her summers in **Taos, New Mexico**, where she gained new inspiration for her art from the rich, colorful expanses of the land and sky. In 1946, a show of hers became the first showing of a woman artist ever held at the **Museum of Modern Art (MoMA)** in New York City. The same year, Stieglitz died, and O'Keeffe moved to New Mexico permanently.

She divided her time between her house in Abiquiu and a ranch outside of town that she had purchased in 1940. She lived simply, growing her own vegetables and grinding wheat flour by hand for bread. Her paintings of cow skulls and bones, adobe buildings, desert scenes, and her studies of Taos Pueblo, an Indian village, are among her most famous works.

In the 1960s, Georgia O'Keeffe had several major showings of her art in cities throughout the United States. In 1970, she was awarded a gold medal from the National Institute of Arts and Letters for her work, and in 1977, she received the **Presidential Medal of Freedom**. Nearly blind in her later years, O'Keeffe continued to paint and sculpt until her death at the age of ninety-eight.

The first woman and the first African American to graduate with a master's degree from the College of Hawaii (now the University of Hawaii), **ALICE BALL** spent her short life using her dazzling scientific mind to improve the lives of others. Creator of the "Ball Method," a revolutionary treatment for **Hansen's disease**, also known as **leprosy**, at a time when there were few other options, she was also the first African American instructor at the college, fighting both gender and racial stereotypes and using her gifts to make an impact.

Ball was born on July 24, 1892, in Seattle, Washington, as one of four children to James Presley and Laura Louise Ball. Alice grew up in a stable, middle-class home. Throughout her school-age years, Alice received top grades in the sciences, carving a path for her future.

She attended the University of Washington to study **pharmaceutical chemistry**, then she earned an additional degree in pharmacy. Her undergraduate work impressed many around the country, especially after she contributed a professional article in the *Journal of the American Chemical Society* titled "Benzoylations in Ether Solution." This was a tremendous accomplishment not only for an African American woman in the early 1900s, but for any woman at the time.

After receiving her Bachelor of Science degree, Ball moved on to the College of Hawaii for her graduate studies. A local doctor, Dr. Harry Hollman, an assistant surgeon at Kalihi Hospital, was looking for assistants to help him research how to isolate active components of chaulmoogra oil, which was used to treat leprosy. At the time, people diagnosed with the infectious disease that causes skin and nerve damage were sent to isolation colonies.

The oil had been used as a topical treatment for centuries, but when physicians attempted to inject the oil or have patients swallow it, it appeared to be ineffective because of its thickness. While working on the research team, Ball discovered a method to make the oil treatment injectable. This was a feat hundreds of other professionals had been working on for years but had not yet achieved. This new method was the only treatment for leprosy that didn't irritate the patient's skin or cause an intense bitter taste through ingestion.

Unfortunately, Ball died unexpectedly on December 31, 1916, at the young age of twenty-four. The research team went on to publish their discovery without giving Ball credit for her major contribution. Arthur Dean, a chemist at the college, continued the work Ball started and named her discovery after himself—dubbing it the "Dean Method" at first; it was later corrected to the Ball Method. The method allowed leprosy patients to be treated in their homes surrounded by their families without going into exile. For over two decades, the treatment was the preferred method for treating the disease.

After more than eighty years, the University of Hawaii recognized Alice Ball's contributions and scientific discovery. Her work improved the lives of suffering individuals who had been isolated from their lives and families while they battled illness.

◆ **MARY PICKFORD** used a childlike and graceful screen presence, as well as a strong knowledge of the movie business, to become one of the most influential people in motion picture history.

Born **Gladys Marie Smith** in Toronto, Canada, Pickford was the eldest child of John and Charlotte Smith. Her father, a laborer, was killed in a work-related accident when Pickford was five. Left destitute, her mother took up sewing and rented a spare room to lodgers to support herself and her three children. One boarder was the stage manager of a Toronto theater company, who hired Pickford and her sister Lottie for roles in his play called *The Silver King*.

Other roles followed for "Baby Gladys Smith," as Pickford was billed, and she spent her childhood either in Toronto or on the road, accompanied by her mother, her sister, and her brother Jack, who was also an actor. When she could no longer find work in theater companies, the fourteen-year-old Pickford went to New York alone and approached famed producer **David Belasco** for a job. He changed her name to Mary Pickford and cast her in his Broadway production of *The Warrens of Virginia*.

At fifteen, Pickford began her film career, working for director **D. W. Griffith** at his Biograph Studios. In 1912, she joined the Famous Players film company, starring in movie versions of such classic stories as *Rebecca of Sunnybrook Farm* and *A Little Princess*. In 1918, she became the first female movie star to head her own production company, when she and her mother formed the **Mary Pickford Film Corporation**.

A year later, Pickford joined D. W. Griffith and movie stars **Charlie Chaplin** and **Douglas Fairbanks** to form the **United Artists** film company. In 1920, Pickford and Fairbanks were married. By then, Pickford had become a multimillionaire; nicknamed "**America's Sweetheart**," she was the most popular actress in movies, mobbed by adoring fans wherever she went. Pickfair, Pickford and Fairbanks' mansion, was one of the most famous homes in Hollywood.

Even as an adult, the petite Pickford played youngsters on the screen, starring as Pollyanna and Little Lord Fauntleroy. She shocked her fans when she had her long, golden hair cut in the 1920s. In 1929, Pickford appeared in her first "talkie," *Coquette*, for which she won an **Academy Award**. After starring in *Secrets* in 1933, Pickford retired from acting to focus on producing, writing, and charity work.

Pickford and Fairbanks divorced in 1936, and soon afterward, she married actor-bandleader **Buddy Rogers**, with whom she adopted two children. They remained together until her death in 1979.

Mary Pickford's last public appearance was at the 1976 Academy Awards, where she received a special Oscar for her contribution to the film industry.

For more than twenty years, **DOROTHY THOMPSON** was the most influential female journalist in the United States.

The oldest of three children to a traveling Methodist minister from the Buffalo, New York area, Thompson lived in five different homes by the time she was twelve years old. She attended Syracuse University and graduated in 1914. She then worked as a publicist for a Buffalo women's suffrage group and later as publicity director for an urban reform organization in Cincinnati.

In her late twenties, Thompson decided to become a journalist, but she could not find a job. Nevertheless, she remained determined and sailed for Europe in 1920; within months, she was filing major news stories for the **International News Service**. During the 1920s, she worked as a **foreign correspondent** for the *Philadelphia Star Ledger* and as chief of Central European Services for the *New York Evening Post*. While working in Berlin, Germany, Thompson met noted American author **Sinclair Lewis**, whom she married in 1928. They had a son in 1930, but as her career skyrocketed during the 1930s, their marriage became strained and the couple divorced in 1942.

Thompson spent the early 1930s writing articles on the political conditions that eventually led to World War II. An interview with future German dictator Adolf Hitler in 1931 was expanded into a 1932 book called *I Saw Hitler!* Although the book enhanced her reputation as a journalist, at the same time, she had seriously underestimated Hitler, believing he was incapable of gaining power. By 1934, the Nazis were in control, and she was expelled from Germany.

In 1936, Thompson began writing a three-times-a-week column called "On the Record" for the *New York Herald Tribune*, interpreting political events for women readers. Syndicated in more than one hundred and fifty newspapers nationwide, it had a readership of seven to eight million people. A monthly column for the *Ladies' Home Journal* and a successful radio program added to her audience.

Before America entered World War II in 1941, Thompson campaigned for U.S. involvement in the Allied cause, and in 1940, she endorsed President Franklin D. Roosevelt for reelection. That stance led to the termination of her contract with the Republican *Herald Tribune* and caused her to switch her column to the more liberal *New York Post*.

During the war, Thompson broadcast a shortwave radio series to Germany, attacking the evils of Nazism and appealing to the humanity of the German people.

After the war, Thompson remained a newspaper columnist, focusing much of her attention on the Middle East. In 1958, she gave up her column, but she continued writing for the *Ladies' Home Journal* about education and family issues.

Dorothy Thompson died of a heart attack in Lisbon, Portugal, in 1961.

Actress, singer, and comedian **HATTIE McDANIEL** built a memorable career in entertainment, and made history, despite the obstacles and prejudice she faced as a Black woman.

Hattie McDaniel was born in Wichita, Kansas, to formerly enslaved parents. After the family moved to Colorado, it became clear that McDaniel had extraordinary talent in singing and acting. After dropping out of school, she toured from town to town, performing with several different groups and ensembles, and soon became one of the first Black women to be broadcast on the radio. However, when the Great Depression started in 1929, most of her performance opportunities disappeared.

McDaniel moved to Los Angeles in 1931, hoping to find more work. She secured a role on a radio show, *The Optimistic Do-Nut Hour*, and soon became a favorite of listeners. Despite her popularity, she was paid so little that she still had to work an additional job as a maid to support herself. She appeared in her first film, *The Golden West*, in 1932, and soon began getting more film roles, though she went uncredited for many of them. However, some members of the Black community objected to Black actors, including McDaniel, only being cast as characters who were servants or enslaved people because the roles perpetuated hurtful stereotypes of African Americans. Groups like the **NAACP** asked Black actors to pressure film studios to stop these practices by refusing to accept these types of roles. However, McDaniel argued that she shouldn't be criticized for earning a living in a world that didn't offer many opportunities to African Americans, saying, "Why should I complain about making $700 a week playing a maid? If I didn't, I'd be making $7 a week being one."

McDaniel was best known for her role in the film adaptation of *Gone with the Wind*. She portrayed Mammy, one of the workers enslaved at Tara, the O'Hara family plantation. McDaniel was not allowed to attend the film's premier in Atlanta, Georgia, because of the state's strict segregation laws. When she attended the Oscars Ceremony—where she became the first Black actor to have been nominated or win an **Academy Award**—she was forced to sit at a segregated table at the side of the room.

McDaniel went on to appear in more than a dozen other films throughout the 1940s. During World War II, she helped organize entertainment at military bases for Black soldiers and performed at United Service Organizations (USO) shows.

Hattie McDaniel died of breast cancer in 1952. Her last wish was to be buried in Hollywood Cemetery but was denied because of her race. However, in the decades after her death, she began receiving more recognition, not only for her talent as a performer but also for her triumphs in the face of brutal racism and discrimination. She has two **Hollywood Walk of Fame** stars and was posthumously inducted into the **Black Filmmakers Hall of Fame** in 1975. In 2006, the U.S. Postal Service released a commemorative stamp in honor of McDaniel.

DOROTHEA LANGE'S photographs chronicled the despair of Americans forced into poverty during the years of the Great Depression. Her powerful images of destitute people helped to create a national awareness of their plight and became classics of documentary photography.

She was born Dorothea Nutzhorn in Hoboken, New Jersey. Her father abandoned the family when she was a young girl, and her mother resumed her maiden name for herself and her children. After graduating from high school in 1913, Lange was determined to become a photographer, although she knew very little about the work. While attending the New York Training School for Teachers, she went to work as an apprentice for portrait photographers and studied with renowned artist-photographer **Clarence H. White**.

In 1918, Lange went to San Francisco, where she worked as a photofinisher and joined a camera club. In 1919, she started a portrait photography business. Lange's studio became a gathering place for many artists, including painter **Maynard Dixon**, whom Lange married in 1920. Throughout the decade, her successful business supported the couple and their two children.

In the early 1930s, Lange abandoned her lucrative career to photograph the victims of the Depression. Her first attempt resulted in one of her most famous photographs titled *White Angel Breadline*, which shows a sad-faced unemployed man staring down at a cup in his hands with his back to the men in line for food. Her photographs of migrant workers for the California State Emergency Relief fund led to the first state-run camps for migrants. In 1935, Lange divorced Dixon and married **Paul Taylor**, an economist who had worked with her on the project.

From 1935 to 1942, Lange traveled around the country photographing rural Americans for the **Farm Security Administration**. Her work was reproduced in numerous magazines and newspapers as well as in books and exhibits, and they had an enormous impact on the public. Her famed photograph *The Migrant Mother*, which depicts a destitute woman holding a baby while two children lean over her shoulders, was published worldwide to raise funds for medical supplies.

During World War II, the government hired Lange to document the mass relocation of Japanese Americans in **internment camps**. In the 1950s, Lange produced photo essays for *Life* magazine and worked with photographer **Edward Steichen** on his remarkable exhibit of people around the world, *The Family of Man*. In 1966, a year after her death, a retrospective exhibition of Lange's work opened at New York's **Museum of Modern Art**. Her study of American women, *The American Country Woman*, was published that year as well.

One of the most inspirational leaders in the struggle for racial justice in America, **SEPTIMA POINSETTE CLARK** dedicated her life to the causes of literacy and voter registration for Black Americans. A schoolteacher for most of her life, Clark believed that education was the key to political power for African Americans. Her **"citizenship schools,"** which combined the teaching of literacy and voting rights instruction, spread throughout the southeastern United States and motivated thousands of southern Blacks to register to vote.

Septima Poinsette Clark's father was born into slavery on the plantation of Joel Poinsette, a former American ambassador to Mexico. Her mother grew up in Haiti. As Clark recalled, she learned patience from her father and courage from her mother who "wasn't afraid of anyone." Both parents valued education above all, and Septima graduated from a private secondary school in Charleston, South Carolina, that trained Black educators.

Since Charleston's public schools barred African Americans from teaching, Clark began her career in 1916 on isolated Johns Island, where she taught impoverished fourth through eighth graders to read and write in a one-room school.

Clark would go on to teach in Columbia, South Carolina, where she began working with the **NAACP** to secure equal pay for Black teachers, who usually received about half the salary of white teachers.

In the 1950s, Clark lost her job when the South Carolina legislature barred teachers from belonging to the NAACP; that prompted her to move, in 1956, to the Highlander Folk School, an integrated school and social activism center in Tennessee. There, in 1957, Clark began opening her citizenship schools so that African Americans could meet the literacy requirements for voter registration.

Clark traveled across the South by bus to recruit new citizenship schoolteachers, refusing to sit in the "colored" section when she traveled. By 1970, she had helped to coordinate the registration of more than one million Black voters. The election to the U.S. Congress in 1972 of the first two African Americans from the South since Reconstruction—**Barbara Jordan** (see no. 80) of Texas and **Andrew Young** of Georgia—and the many who followed them, is due in large part to Clark's tireless efforts to bolster the political power of African Americans.

Clark was also an active member of the **Southern Christian Leadership Conference (SCLC)**. When Clark died in 1987, Joseph E. Lowery, president of the SCLC, compared her to **Harriet Tubman**, who had helped hundreds of enslaved people escape to freedom during the 1850s. Lowery declared, "Septima Poinsette Clark led her people to freedom through journeys from the darkness of illiteracy to the shining light of literacy."

Known as New York City's first Puerto Rican librarian, **PURA BELPRÉ** quickly became a guiding light for **Spanish-speaking New Yorkers** looking to integrate into New York's culture. Hosting bilingual story times and infusing Latino culture into her stories and puppet shows, she catalyzed a movement for inclusivity and openness in the library systems and local resources, opening doors of possibility for Spanish-speaking families while honoring their rich culture.

Pura Belpré grew up in **Puerto Rico** and attended the University of Puerto Rico to study to become a teacher. However, when Pura traveled to New York City to attend her sister's wedding, she decided to make her home in the city. Soon, she was recruited by the New York Public Library system; the organization had just started recruiting young women from diverse backgrounds to connect with the city's changing demographics. At the time, New York's Puerto Rican population was growing rapidly, and Belpré could connect with them in a way that other librarians could not.

Belpré became the **New York Public Library**'s first Puerto Rican librarian. She traveled all over the city hosting bilingual story times—a first for New York residents. Belpré used puppets to tell her stories, which captivated her young audiences, and she infused her events with rich **Latino folklore** and culture. Before she arrived, many Spanish-speaking residents avoided the public library system, thinking it only catered to English-speaking people. Belpré's programming and storytelling soon reestablished the city's libraries as welcoming places for residents of all backgrounds.

Years later, Belpré wrote several books. It bothered her that Spanish-speaking people and Puerto Ricans specifically didn't have good representation in children's literature. Her writing used Puerto Rican folklore to entertain youngsters. Her most famous book was *Pérez and Martina*, a love story involving a rat and a cockroach.

Belpré retired from the New York Public Library in 1968, after several decades of service. Belpré passed away on July 1, 1982, in New York City, but her legacy in storytelling, activism, and literature lives on. The **American Library Association** awards the **Pura Belpré Medal** each year to a Latino/Latina writer and illustrator whose work celebrates and shares Latino cultural experiences. Today, librarians credit Belpré with opening the door for all types of Spanish resources available for residents today to ensure they receive as much of a benefit from the local resource as everyone else.

MARGARET MITCHELL is the author of *Gone with the Wind*, the most popular novel of the twentieth century. Mitchell's epic story of the American South, the **American Civil War**, and the **Reconstruction** era sold more than a million copies during the first year of its publication in 1936 and continues to sell widely today. After the movie version of Mitchell's only novel was released in 1939, *Gone with the Wind's* hold on popular culture reached an unprecedented level. When the movie was first broadcast on television in 1976, it drew some 110 million viewers, which was at that time the largest audience in TV history.

The daughter of a prominent Atlanta couple, Margaret Mitchell was steeped by her mother and grandmother in the history of the American Civil War and Reconstruction era she wrote about. As a young girl, she accompanied them on tours of defunct Georgia plantations and heard

them talk "about the world those people lived in, such a secure world, and how it had exploded beneath them." *Gone with the Wind* originated in Mitchell's desire to recall that explosion and its consequences.

Having been a debutante and society lady, Mitchell began her writing career as a reporter for the *Atlanta Journal*. During her convalescence at home from an injury, she finished reading all the books in her library, and her husband remarked, "It looks to me, Peggy, as though you'll have to write a book yourself if you're going to have anything to read." This began Mitchell's ten-year effort to produce *Gone with the Wind*.

Mitchell's massive novel tells the story of the charming, willful, and spoiled **Scarlett O'Hara**, and her fight to save her family's plantation, **Tara**, from ruin during and after the Civil War. Scarlett's romance with the story's main male character, the roguish **Rhett Butler**, captivated readers who both loved Scarlett for her strength in the face of adversity and reviled her for her heartlessness and selfishness. What sets *Gone with the Wind* apart from so many previous novels is that Mitchell centered her story around a complex and flawed female character who takes control of her life, challenging traditional notions of how women should behave.

Margaret Mitchell ended her novel with a wealthy Scarlett alone and friendless but determined to triumph over adversity once again. Mitchell steadfastly refused the popular demand for a sequel to resolve the suspense over Scarlett's fate that concludes *Gone with the Wind*.

Sadly, Mitchell died in an accident caused by an out-of-control taxicab in 1949. Despite her tragically shortened life, Mitchell still managed to produce one of the most popular books in American history.

One of the key leaders of the Civil Rights Movement of the 1950s and 1960s, **ELLA BAKER** spent a lifetime battling racial injustice. An influential member of three major civil rights organizations, she was also an organizer of many small grassroots community groups that achieved significant victories in the battle for civil rights.

Born in Norfolk, Virginia, Baker grew up in North Carolina on land where her grandparents had been enslaved. After graduating as class valedictorian from Shaw University in Raleigh, North Carolina, in 1927, Baker moved to New York City to look for work.

She took jobs as a waitress and a factory worker, and then she began to write for Black publications.

In 1932, she co-organized the **Young Negro Cooperative League**, a consumer group dedicated to helping the disadvantaged during the Great Depression. During the 1940s, Baker traveled throughout the segregated South to organize branches of the **NAACP**. She became known for her determination and fearlessness in an atmosphere of racial violence, in which African Americans could be killed for simply trying to register to vote.

During the Montgomery, Alabama, bus boycott of 1955–1957, which began after Rosa Parks' famous refusal to sit in the segregated section in the back of a bus, Baker organized assistance for the boycotters and other African Americans who had suffered reprisals for their civil rights activities. In 1958, she helped to establish the **SCLC** to widen the opposition to racial injustice in the South. While Martin Luther King Jr. became the group's inspirational leader, it was Baker who managed the SCLC organization, which grew into sixty-five affiliates in various southern cities.

During a wave of sit-ins by Black college students in the winter of 1960, Baker saw an opportunity to harness the students' dedication and enthusiasm for social activism. She helped establish the **Student Nonviolent Coordinating Committee (SNCC)** and taught members how to organize protests and coordinate voter registration drives.

Eventually, Baker's efforts on behalf of SNCC and the **Mississippi Freedom Democratic Party**, which she formed to challenge the power of the all-white state Democratic Party, led to the landmark passage of the **Voting Rights Act of 1965**. This legislation, which guaranteed voting protection for all U.S. citizens, is one of the major achievements of the Civil Rights Movement.

Those who knew Baker called her "Fundi," a Swahili term for a person who bequeaths knowledge to the next generation. In light of Ella Baker's lifetime contribution to the cause of civil rights, that seems to be a fitting moniker.

Considered Hollywood's first **Chinese American film star**, **ANNA MAY WONG** broke into California's sprouting film industry in the early 1900s and cut a path for herself and her career where none existed. She endured discrimination and typecasting over her entire career, but she continued to fight for **Asian American representation** in the white-dominated **Hollywood film industry**.

Anna May Wong was born in **Los Angeles, California**, on January 3, 1905, in the **Chinatown neighborhood**. Wong was born to a **Chinese immigrant family** with ethnic ties to Taishan, China, where her grandfather had emigrated from before Anna's father was born. Her parents owned and operated a laundromat, where she and her sister worked while attending school.

American film production made a major shift in the early 1900s, moving from New York to Los Angeles, and Wong was immediately infatuated with the industry. She

would often skip school and use her lunch money to go to the theater. She knew she was destined to be a star, and without her parents' permission, she auditioned for and landed her first role as an extra in *The Red Lantern* in 1919. After earning several additional extra and supporting roles, and dropping out of high school to pursue acting, she received her first leading role in *The Toll of the Sea* in 1922, one of the first films ever produced in **Technicolor**.

Wong worked in Hollywood for many years, and she was most often typecast into stereotypical Asian roles and was discriminated against in the white-dominated industry. She protested when studios would cast white actresses to portray Asian characters, while they shoved Asian actresses into supporting or background roles. In the mid-1920s, she decided to head to Europe to work in theater and films, finding great success there. However, back in Hollywood, **Paramount Studios** contacted Wong, promising her attractive leading roles if she'd return to the States. She was awarded prominent roles after she returned, but she still felt they were stereotypical and often inaccurate cultural representations. In the 1950s, she became the first Asian American to perform as the lead character on a television show when she starred in *The Gallery of Madame Liu-Tsong*, a mystery series following a Chinese art dealer.

Anna May Wong died on February 3, 1961, at the age of fifty-six after suffering a heart attack. Up until her death, she was still pursuing roles and fighting for accurate representation and fair opportunity for Asian American actresses. Today, Wong is seen as a trailblazer for actresses of diverse backgrounds, many of whom are still working to level the playing field in the entertainment industry.

A choreographer, dancer, teacher, and author, **AGNES DE MILLE** was one of the most influential figures in American dance. She combined classical and modern dance with the spirited rhythms of American folk dances and helped to transform American musical theater by bringing the beauty of ballet to a wider audience.

De Mille was a member of a very well-known American theatrical family, which included her father, playwright and director **William de Mille**, and her uncle, film producer-director **Cecil B. de Mille**. Born in New York City on September 18, 1905, she grew up in Hollywood, and at the age of ten, after seeing the great dancer **Anna Pavlova** perform, was determined to become a dancer herself. Her parents discouraged her from considering a stage career and initially refused her dancing lessons, but eventually they relented and she began to study ballet.

To please her parents, she deferred her dream of becoming a dancer to attend the University of California, Los Angeles (UCLA). Following graduation, de Mille went to New York City to establish her career as a dancer and choreographer. She achieved little success, though, because Broadway producers were not interested in her attempt to incorporate classical and American folk elements in her dances in place of the conventional chorus-line dancing, which was popular at the time.

In the early 1930s, a frustrated de Mille went to Europe, where she studied, worked, and performed for a number of years to much greater success. In 1939, she returned to the United States and was asked to join the newly formed **New York Ballet Theatre**, which would later become the **American Ballet Theatre**. With this group, de Mille choreographed *Black Ritual*, the first ballet performed entirely by Black dancers in a classic American ballet company. Her ballet, *Rodeo*, a celebration of the American West with music by **Aaron Copland**, would become a landmark in dance and theater history, featuring an innovative mixture of folk dancing, modern dance, and classical ballet.

De Mille also made history with her dances for the Rodgers and Hammerstein musical *Oklahoma!* The show featured an integration of story, song, and dance for the first time in a musical comedy and ushered in a new era of sophistication and artistry in musical theater. De Mille would also go on to choreograph such classical musicals as *Carousel* and *Brigadoon.*

In the 1960s, de Mille became the cofounder and president of the **Society of Stage Directors and Choreographers**. In 1973, she founded the **Heritage Dance Theatre**, which was devoted to traditional American dance. De Mille's achievement in transforming American dance was acknowledged with a Kennedy Center Award in 1980 and a **National Medal of Arts** in 1986.

OVETA CULP HOBBY was one of the most prominent women in the U.S. government during the 1940s and 1950s. As the first head of the **Women's Army Corps (WACs)** and later as **secretary of the Department of Health, Education, and Welfare (HEW)**, she opened important doors for women in the military and in government. Hobby's appointment to the HEW post made her the second American woman to hold a position in the Cabinet of the United States.

Born in Killeen, Texas, Oveta Culp was a gifted student who followed her father into the legal profession. After graduating from the University of Texas Law School at the young age of twenty, she became an assistant city attorney in Houston and parliamentarian for the Texas Legislature. At twenty-six, she married **William Hobby**, a former Texas governor and publisher of the *Houston Post*.

During World War II, Hobby went to Washington to head the newly formed women's division of the War Department Bureau of Public Relations. There, she drafted plans for the formation of a women's auxiliary to the all-male army, which eventually resulted in the formation of the WACs.

Hobby was given the responsibility of heading the new corps. Initially restricted to fifty-four army jobs such as secretaries and nurses, the WAC eventually took on 185 more jobs under Hobby's leadership, including war planning, mapmaking, and code work, areas previously restricted to men. Hobby also initiated a program to recruit African American women for the officer corps.

By 1943, Hobby was overseeing the activities of more than one hundred thousand WACs in a wide variety of noncombatant positions, and her efforts made her the second most important woman in the American war effort, second only to Eleanor Roosevelt.

Hobby was made a colonel in the army and received the **Distinguished Service Medal** for her war work.

In 1953, **President Dwight D. Eisenhower** appointed Hobby the first head of the newly created Department of Health, Education, and Welfare. She oversaw the Public Health Service, the Food and Drug Administration, the Office of Education, and the Bureau of Old Age and Survivors Insurance. Subsequently, in 1955, she was charged with supervising the important national distribution of Jonas Salk's polio vaccine.

Forced to resign her position and return to Texas to care for her ailing husband, Hobby took control of the *Houston Post*. She helped the publication develop into one of the nation's leading metropolitan daily newspapers and become part of a media empire of radio and television stations.

Oveta Culp Hobby helped pave the way for women in both military and civilian life. With her organizational and business skills, she proved that women could direct large corporations and serve with distinction in the most important positions in government.

Aviator **JACQUELINE COCHRAN** once described her career as having gone "from sawdust to stardust." That is an apt description of a woman who spent her childhood in poverty, but whose aeronautic accomplishments helped pave the way for women combat fliers, test pilots, and astronauts.

Born somewhere in Florida into poverty, Cochran was an ambitious girl who began working from a young age. Educated only through the second grade, Cochran worked in cotton mills in Georgia for six cents an hour on twelve-hour shifts when she was eight years old. To escape her destitution, the teenage Cochran trained as a beautician and attended nursing school in Montgomery, Alabama. She later went to Pensacola, Florida, where she became part owner of a beauty shop.

In 1929, Cochran moved to New York City, where she gained a job at the Saks Fifth Avenue beauty salon. There, she met millionaire **Floyd Bostwick Oldum**, whom she eventually married. Oldum helped Cochran start her own cosmetics company, and in 1932, he encouraged her to take up flying to help her sell her products around the country. She loved flying from the outset, and in 1933, she earned her commercial pilot's license.

Cochran flew in a number of airplane races—in many as the first woman participant—and by 1939, she was setting international speed, altitude, and distance records. In 1940, she became president of the **Ninety-Nines**, a female aviation group founded by **Amelia Earhart**. During World War II, to prove that women could handle heavy aircraft as well as men, she became the first woman to pilot a bomber across the Atlantic.

Cochran and twenty-five American women pilots volunteered in the **British Air Transport Auxiliary**, ferrying combat aircraft from North America. When the United States established a similar **Women's Auxiliary Ferrying Squadron**, Cochran was put in charge of recruiting and training female pilots for the **Women Airforce Service Pilots (WASP)**. Eventually more than one thousand WASPs delivered twelve thousand planes to the war zone in Europe.

After the war, Cochran joined the **Air Force Reserves**, and in 1953, she broke the world speed records for both men and women in a Sabre jet. The same year, she was the first woman to fly faster than the speed of sound (Mach 1). In 1964, Cochran became the fastest woman alive, when she flew at 1,429 mph—twice the speed of sound.

In 1970, Cochran retired as a colonel in the Air Force Reserves. The following year, she was inducted into the **American Aviation Hall of Fame**, becoming the only living woman to receive that honor.

KATHARINE HEPBURN is recognized as one of the most distinguished and unique movie actresses in the history of motion pictures. In a career that spanned more than fifty years, Hepburn dazzled audiences with her portrayals of strong, spirited, independent women, and won **four Academy Awards**—the most achieved by any single actor.

Born in Hartford, Connecticut, Hepburn was the daughter of a well-to-do surgeon and a mother who scandalized conservative Hartford by working for such controversial causes as birth control and women's suffrage. The Hepburn children were encouraged to be independent, self-reliant, and inquisitive. She was educated by private tutors, and at sixteen, she entered Bryn Mawr College, where she studied drama and appeared in school productions.

After graduating in 1928, Hepburn moved to New York to pursue a theatrical career. Her early stage appearances, however, were dismal failures. Her acting was artificial, her voice was high and tinny, and she suffered from stage fright. Her breakthrough came in 1932, when she was cast as the queen of the Amazons in *The Warrior's Husband* on Broadway. Her beauty, athletic grace, and performance as an emancipated, spirited woman captivated audiences.

Hepburn's stage success led to movie work in Hollywood, where she received good reviews in her first film, *A Bill of Divorcement* (1932). She went on to attain stardom in a long series of memorable roles, portraying such characters as feisty Jo March in *Little Women* (1933), icy socialite Tracy Lord in *The Philadelphia Story* (1940), a world-famous political commentator in *Woman of the Year* (1942), a strait-laced missionary in *The African Queen* (1951), and Eleanor of

Aquitaine in *The Lion in Winter* (1968), for which she won her third Oscar. Hepburn's other Oscar-winning performances were in the films *Morning Glory* (1933), *Guess Who's Coming to Dinner* (1967), and *On Golden Pond* (1981).

After an early brief marriage to Philadelphia socialite **Ludlow Ogden Smith** and subsequent divorce, Hepburn never remarried.

However, beginning in the early 1940s, she became romantically involved with her *Woman of the Year* costar, **Spencer Tracy**. They made nine films together, and although many inside Hollywood knew of their long-time affair, it was kept secret from the public because Tracy's Roman Catholicism was an impediment to his getting a divorce. Even after his death in 1967, Hepburn would never comment publicly on their twenty-five-year relationship.

Mary Golda Ross was the first **American Indian woman engineer**. Known as one of the many **hidden figures** of **mid-century America**'s engineering and mathematics disciplines, she built an impressive career in engineering, working on teams as the only woman, and she used her retirement to guide and inspire other American Indians to pursue their dreams in the sciences.

Mary Golda Ross was born on August 9, 1908, in Park Hill, Oklahoma. She was one of five children and was born into the **Cherokee Nation**; her great-grandfather was the well-known Chief John Ross. After completing primary and secondary education, at sixteen years old Ross went on to Northeastern State Teacher's College, where she earned a degree in mathematics at twenty years old. She started teaching math and science in Oklahoma before working as a statistical clerk for the **Bureau of Indian Affairs** in Washington, DC. The organization relocated her to advising at the Santa Fe Indian School, and during her time there, she chipped away at classes to receive her master's degree in mathematics at Colorado State Teachers College. While there, she also took every astronomy course the college offered as she was enamored with astronomy and the stars.

In 1941, Ross moved to California where she made history as the first American Indian woman engineer. At the time, many companies were hiring women for positions that were traditionally filled by men due to the decline in workforce because of **World War II**. She got a job working for Lockheed Corporation and began by designing fighter planes. When the war concluded, many women were released from their positions, but Ross stayed on. Lockheed even sponsored her professional **engineering** certification at UCLA. In the early 1950s, Ross was one of forty founding members of Lockheed's top-secret development group Skunk Works. She was the only woman and only American Indian engineer on the team.

During her career, Ross researched various defense systems, satellite orbits, and systems intended for manned space flights. She also coauthored the *NASA Planetary Flight Handbook Vol. III*, which explored details of space travel between Mars and Venus. Much of her work assisted engineers and experts in planning for future **space travel**.

Ross retired from Lockheed in the early 1970s, but she didn't stop building opportunity for other American Indians. She was a member of the **Society of Women Engineers**, and she spent her free time recruiting and mentoring women and Native Americans in the opportunities and possibilities for science, technology, engineering, and math (STEM) careers.

Mary Golda Ross passed away on April 29, 2008, at ninety-nine years old. Before her death, she attended the opening ceremonies of the **National Museum of the American Indian** in Washington, DC. After her death, she left a $400,000 endowment to the museum, knowing that the organization would continue to support American Indian culture and growth in society today.

Creator of the **Apgar Score System**, **VIRGINIA APGAR** was a pioneering medical professional who dedicated her career to understanding birth defects and infant mortality rates to a degree that had never been accomplished before. Surrounded by men in the field of medicine, Virginia created space for herself to leave a mark on modern medicine.

Virginia Apgar was born in Westfield, New Jersey, on June 7, 1909, as the youngest of three children. For her entire life, she was known for her endless enthusiasm and energy. She took to the sciences early, and she knew she wanted to practice medicine by the time she was in high school. In 1925, she enrolled in Mount Holyoke College to study zoology. Working to support herself through school, she still made time to enjoy her college experience.

While studying and impressing her professors, she also participated in seven sports teams, performed in the theater productions, contributed to the school paper, and played the violin in the school orchestra (which she had played in since childhood). She graduated with her degree in 1929 and went on to the College of Physicians and Surgeons at Columbia University. One of very few women in the program, she completed her medical doctorate (MD) in 1933, but as she was about to begin her surgical training at Presbyterian Hospital, a mentor redirected her to **anesthesiology**, fearing for the job landscape for women during the **Great Depression**.

Apgar dove into the discipline, studying under some of the best doctors in the country. After her residency, she returned to Presbyterian Hospital to lead the anesthesia division, becoming the first woman to do so at that hospital. Over several years, Apgar built a reputable anesthesia program there, providing training and education and leading research to refine the discipline.

Apgar had a growing interest in studying infant mortality rates. In the early 1950s, through her research, Apgar developed a scoring system to evaluate the health of newborn babies just after delivery. The system's results soon became known as "Apgar scores." Today, her **Apgar evaluation** is standard practice in delivery rooms all over the world, helping others to assess newborn health and understand birth defects to improve quality of life and understanding.

Apgar never stopped working. She continued with many of her hobbies—similar to her college years—and she continued to grow in her role as an advocate for birth defect research and education. She passed away on August 7, 1974, after a long fight with liver disease. For her contributions to science, she was featured on a U.S. postage stamp in 1994. Virginia Apgar was not outwardly involved in gender equality or feminism movements in her lifetime, but she didn't allow traditional gender stereotypes in the field of medicine keep her from leaving a lasting impact on humans all around the world.

Comedian **LUCILLE BALL** was the most popular and influential woman in the history of early television. The star and co-creator of *I Love Lucy*, Ball is still entertaining millions of people around the world through the syndication of the show in reruns more than fifty years after its debut.

Born near Jamestown, New York, Lucille Ball left home at the age of fifteen to pursue an acting career in New York City. In acting school, she was repeatedly told that she had no talent and should return home. Determined to succeed in show business, she worked as a waitress and a model before getting national attention for the first time in 1933 as the Chesterfield cigarette girl.

Ball was invited to Hollywood to try her luck in movies, and during the late 1930s and early 1940s, she enjoyed modest success as an actress in a variety of comedies and dramas.

In 1940, she married Cuban bandleader **Desi Arnaz**, whom she had met while the two were making a film. In 1950, the couple formed **Desilu Productions** to enable them to work together in movies and television. Ball and Arnaz tried to sell a husband-and-wife comedy series starring themselves to a TV network, but executives were convinced that the public would not accept the Cuban-born Arnaz as Ball's on-screen husband.

To prove the networks wrong, Ball and Arnaz embarked on a nationwide tour, performing their husband-and-wife sketches to live audiences. Finally, they found a sponsor for their concept, and *I Love Lucy* debuted on CBS on October 15, 1951.

From 1951 to 1957, nearly forty million viewers each week watched the zany antics of **"America's Favorite Redhead."** *I Love Lucy* established the basic situation comedy (sitcom) as a major television entertainment form for future generations of viewers. Since Ball and Arnaz controlled the production of the show, they held the residual rights to reruns, which meant that when the show went into syndication, they became enormously wealthy.

Ball and Arnaz's collaboration ended with their divorce in 1960. In 1962, Ball bought Arnaz's share in Desilu and became sole head of the company. This made her the first woman to head a major Hollywood studio.

While busy as an executive, Ball continued to perform on television as well as on stage and the big screen. She had two additional television series—*The Lucy Show* and *Here's Lucy*—but neither one captured the total magic of *I Love Lucy*.

With her work on *I Love Lucy*, Lucille Ball established a format for success, both as a performer and as a business executive. Numerous television personalities and executives have tried for more than fifty years to duplicate her success but all have fallen short of the mark.

Known as the "First Lady of Physics," **CHIEN-SHIUNG WU** was lucky to receive an education as a young girl in China in the early 1900s. Wu didn't waste this opportunity for education, and she didn't place limits on where her mind could take her. Enduring gender discrimination and distance from her family, Wu imprinted herself on the field of physics and created a path for female physicists to follow in her footsteps.

Chien-Shiung Wu was born in Liuhe, China, on May 31, 1912, as the middle child—the family's single daughter between two sons. Wu's father, a progressive thinker who believed girls should receive an education just like boys, founded the Mingde Women's Vocational Continuing School. After her primary education was complete, Wu attended the National Central University where she earned a degree in physics.

A mentor encouraged her to move to the United States to continue her physics education. After sailing to **San Francisco** in 1936, she enrolled at the University of California, Berkeley and graduated with her PhD in 1940.

Two years later, Wu married Luke Chia-Liu Yuan, a classmate at Berkeley. They moved to the East Coast so Wu could begin teaching at both Princeton, where she was the first woman hired to the physics department, and Smith College. After moving to New York City to teach at Columbia University, Wu was recruited to work on the Manhattan Project—the **U.S. Army**'s secret program to build an atomic bomb during **World War II**. She helped to develop the process for uranium enrichment needed to fuel the bomb.

Wu continued to teach after the war, and she made major contributions to the field of atomic science. She became a U.S. citizen in 1954, and in 1957, two of her colleagues earned the **Nobel Prize in Physics** for their work investigating parity laws. Wu contributed greatly to the research, but her name was left off the distinction—a common occurrence for women in the sciences at the time. She did not take her exclusion lightly. Years later at a Massachusetts Institute of Technology (MIT) symposium, she addressed her audience and asked them whether they thought atoms or nuclei, among other things, would "have any preference for either masculine or feminine treatment." Wu retired from teaching at Columbia University in 1981, and she passed away on February 16, 1997, after a stroke.

Wu did not let gender discrimination deter her from contributing to the field she loved. Although she was snubbed from the Nobel Prize, she collected many other distinguished accomplishments over her career. She was the first woman to be named president of the American Physical Society, was just the seventh woman in history to be inducted into the National Academy of Sciences, and had an asteroid named in her honor in 1990.

A pioneering psychologist, **MAMIE PHIPPS CLARK** spent most of her career studying the psychology and identity of Black children growing up in a segregated America. Her work provided pivotal support in desegregating America's public school system in the 1950s.

Mamie Phipps Clark was born in **Hot Springs, Arkansas**, on October 18, 1917, to a British West Indian father, who was a practicing physician, and her mother, who assisted her husband's practice. Throughout her childhood, Clark was educated in segregated schools. She was incredibly bright and was offered scholarships to two schools.

She elected to attend **Howard University** for her undergraduate studies, one of the most prominent **Historically Black Colleges and Universities (HBCUs)** in the nation. Clark enrolled in mathematics and physics courses, but she was soon convinced to switch to psychology after she met her future husband and psychology student, Kenneth Clark. The two eloped in their senior year of college. In 1938, Mamie graduated magna cum laude with her bachelor of science degree, and she was admitted into Howard's psychology graduate program.

The summer after she graduated, she began working as a secretary in a local law office, where she was exposed to the ongoing legal work of people like **Thurgood Marshall** and **William Hastie**, who were fighting for African American civil rights in America. Clark went on to study for her PhD at Columbia University, becoming the first African American woman to earn a doctorate from the university and only the second African American just after her husband.

Clark's research focused on how young African American children adopt identities based on their race, and how that aspect of themselves is at play in society. She worked closely with her husband on studies that led to pioneering research, which are still cited and respected in modern psychology.

One of the most well-known aspects of their work were the infamous **doll tests**. The Clarks would work with Black children and show them two identical dolls—the only difference was that one would be Black and the other would be white—and then they would ask them a series of questions regarding the dolls, such as which one was "nice," which was "bad," and which one they wanted to play with. The experiments revealed that racial segregation had drastic, adverse effects on Black children's identity and self-esteem, which was counterproductive to their learning environments.

The Clarks' experiment played a pivotal role in the **Supreme Court**'s 1954 decision of **Brown v. Board of Education**—a landmark court case that decided **racial segregation** in public schools went against the **U.S. Constitution**.

Clark and her husband devoted much of their careers to offering psychological services to underserved communities. Mamie Clark died at her home in New York on August 11, 1983, at sixty-six years old. Her deep dive into the effects of race, segregation, and discrimination acted as a springboard for future psychologists to discover even more about the effects of discrimination on development and identity.

In 1963, **KATHARINE GRAHAM** was suddenly forced to succeed her husband as president and publisher of the *Washington Post*. Defying expectations, Graham built the newspaper into an influential and respected publication, and she became the most powerful woman in American journalism.

Born in New York City, Graham was the daughter of wealthy investment banker **Eugene Meyer**, who in 1933, purchased the struggling *Washington Post*. After Graham's graduation from the University of Chicago that same year, she worked as a reporter in San Francisco before joining the editorial department of the *Post*. In 1940, she married attorney Philip Graham, who, after his service in World War II, assumed the position of publisher of the *Post*.

Philip Graham helped his father-in-law build the business, and then in 1948, Graham and Katharine bought the *Post* from her father. In the early 1960s, the *Post* purchased *Newsweek* magazine, expanded the radio and television operations of the company, and helped to establish an international news service. During her marriage, Katharine Graham largely retired from journalism to raise her three children and become a prominent Washington, DC, society hostess.

In 1963, Philip Graham, who suffered from alcoholism and mental illness, died by suicide. Suddenly, with no executive training, Katharine Graham found herself in charge of the publishing empire. Graham surprised her doubters, however, by becoming a bold decision-maker and business leader.

In an effort to improve the day-to-day leadership at the paper, Graham hired the highly regarded **Ben Bradlee** as the new managing editor. In 1971, she gave Bradlee the go-ahead to publish the **Pentagon Papers**, the secret government documents that revealed the truth about American involvement in Vietnam, which first appeared in the *New York Times*. The decision to do so was a milestone event in protecting freedom of the press, and the *Post's* action was subsequently ruled legal in a U.S. Supreme Court case.

One year later, the **Watergate** scandal emerged, with *Post* reporters **Bob Woodward** and **Carl Bernstein** breaking the story about the connection between a burglary at Washington's Watergate complex and political corruption in the White House. These revelations ultimately led to President Richard Nixon's resignation.

Graham encouraged and financed the Watergate coverage and withstood an all-out White House attack to discredit the *Post* and its investigation. In 1973, the newspaper was awarded a **Pulitzer Prize** for meritorious public service for its coverage of the scandal.

Graham next passed the day-to-day management of the *Post* on to her son Donny in 1979 but remained chair of the board until 1991. In 1998, she published her autobiography titled *Personal History*, which won her a **Pulitzer Prize**.

Katharine Graham died in 2001 of complications after sustaining injuries due to a fall.

The first African American woman to work at **National Aeronautics and Space Administration (NASA)** as a scientist, **KATHERINE JOHNSON** was one of the preeminent **hidden figures** of NASA's early years in space travel and mathematics. Using her brilliant mind and sharp determination, Katherine opened doors for women of color—and women in general—to receive rightful recognition and opportunity in technical fields.

Katherine Johnson was born on August 26, 1918, in White Sulphur Springs, West Virginia. From a very young age, she showed incredible skill with numbers and computing. At just thirteen years old, she started attending math classes at West Virginia State College (now West Virginia State University), a nearby HBCU. She went on to receive her undergraduate degree in mathematics there in 1937, and soon after, she began her teaching career.

In 1939, West Virginia began integrating their graduate schools, and Johnson was one of the first three Black students and the only woman to be selected by West Virginia University to attend. She enrolled in their mathematics program, but she left before completing it to start a family with her husband.

In 1953, Johnson began her career in space mathematics after joining the West Area Computing Unit at the **National Advisory Committee for Aeronautics (NACA)**, the precursor to the **NASA**. Johnson's group was a segregated team of Black women mathematicians who completed very complex equations for the organization's engineers. Although the women of the West Area Computing Unit were providing incredibly important information for the success of the program, they were still forced to use different restrooms and dining areas from their white colleagues. This formal **segregation** ended with the formation of NASA in 1958.

Once the organization became NASA, Johnson joined the Space Task Group, where she worked as part of the **Mercury program**. During the program, Johnson made numerous pivotal contributions. During the *Freedom 7* space flight, she correctly calculated the path that successfully placed astronaut **Alan B. Shepard Jr.** into space—the first U.S. astronaut to travel there. Just one year later, astronaut **John Glenn** famously requested that Johnson double-check the machine computations for his flight path as he didn't fully trust the equipment. Glenn's flight was a success—and the calculations were correct—allowing him to safely become the first American astronaut to orbit Earth.

Johnson spent decades working for NASA. Among many other projects after Project Mercury, she assisted on the *Apollo 11* mission, which took the first humans to the moon in 1969. She retired from her work at NASA in 1986.

As years past, the contributions of Johnson and her female colleagues began to gain more recognition. In 2015, President Barack Obama awarded her the Presidential Medal of Freedom for her work. She and her team were also the subject of a well-known book and film titled *Hidden Figures*, starring actress Taraji P. Henson as Johnson.

Katherine Johnson passed away on February 24, 2020, at the age of 101.

◆ Nobel Prize-winning biochemist **GERTRUDE B. ELION** was a pioneer in the scientific discovery of drugs to treat cancer. Her research increased scientists' understanding of how cells function and led to the development of medications to treat infections and prevent transplant organ rejection.

Born in New York City, the daughter of Russian and Polish immigrants, Gertrude B. Elion was an exceptional student who graduated from high school at the age of fifteen. During her senior year, she witnessed the painful death of her grandfather from stomach cancer and vowed to become a cancer researcher.

After graduating from Hunter College in 1937, Elion was turned down from jobs as a research chemist because she was a woman. Instead, she worked as a lab assistant, food analyst, and high school science teacher while completing her master's degree in chemistry at night.

During World War II, job opportunities for women increased in the United States as men left for military service, and Elion earned a job as a researcher with the **Wellcome Research Laboratories** in Tuckahoe, New York. In 1967, she became head of Wellcome's **Department of Experimental Therapy**, a position she occupied until her retirement in 1983.

Together, Elion and her close friend and colleague **George Hitchings** began the research that would produce the first drugs specifically designed for cancer therapy. By studying the workings of cancer cells, harmful bacteria, and viruses, they had hoped to discover the differences between abnormal and normal cells. In doing so, they would try to determine whether certain chemicals could destroy the abnormal cells without harming healthy ones. Their goal was to control and eradicate cancers and harmful infections.

Elion's research into childhood leukemia led to the development of a drug that proved effective in treating the disease. Before her discovery, there were no effective drugs for children with leukemia, but with the medication she developed, almost 80 percent of children with acute leukemia could be cured. Elion went on to develop drugs that helped to prevent the body from rejecting kidney transplants, as well as drugs that treated viral infections, such as gout and herpes. Based in part on her research, scientists Elion and Hitchings would also develop the drug **AZT**, or azidothymidine, the first effective medication used to treat **acquired immunodeficiency syndrome**, or **AIDS**.

In 1988, Elion and Hitchings received the **Nobel Prize for Medicine**. Elion dealt with the acclaim she received with characteristic practicality. "The Nobel Prize is fine," she declared, "but the drugs I've developed are rewards in themselves." Elion had realized her dream of helping those suffering from cancer and other diseases, while overcoming the prejudice that had limited women's roles as scientific researchers.

JANE C. WRIGHT—a successful African American female physician—was a pioneer in **early cancer research** and **chemotherapy** treatments. Because of her brilliance and dedication, millions of cancer patients around the world are provided with advanced technologies and treatment programs to improve their chances of survival each year.

Jane C. Wright was born on November 20, 1919, in **New York City**. Her father—Dr. Louis Wright, a physician—was the one of the first African Americans to graduate from **Harvard Medical School**. Her father served as an inspiration for her, and in young adulthood, she began pursuing her own career in medicine.

She attended New York Medical College and completed residencies at several local hospitals before joining her father at Harlem Hospital, where he was chief resident and where he founded and directed the hospital's Cancer Research Foundation. At the time, chemotherapy was thought of as a last resort in cancer treatments, but the father–daughter pair focused their research on cancer-fighting chemicals. In 1951, Wright published her findings on the use of the chemotherapy drug **methotrexate**, which was successful in treating breast cancer. Her research and discovery opened a path for current and future physicians to advance the science of chemotherapy and cancer treatments.

At the young age of thirty-three, Wright was appointed head of the Cancer Research Foundation after her father's death in 1952. She was also a founding member of the American Society of Clinical Oncology (ASCO), which had a goal of making cancer research and discoveries accessible to doctors everywhere in order to improve patient outlook and lives.

In 1967, Wright was named associate dean and professor of surgery at New York Medical College, making her the highest-ranked African American woman at a national medical institution at a time when there were only hundreds of practicing African American women physicians in the country. While working there, she continued her research and development of innovative cancer treatments. In 1971, Wright became the first woman to sit as president of the New York Cancer Society.

During her career, Wright published hundreds of research papers on cancer research and treatments, which impacted and supported the advancement of available options for patients all over the world. She retired from practicing medicine in 1987, and she passed away on February 19, 2013, at the age of ninety-three.

MARIE MAYNARD DALY was the first Black woman in U.S. history to earn a PhD in the field of **chemistry**. She dedicated her career and life to understanding life around us, and her contributions to the field have improved healthcare and society's understanding of the human body. As a woman and an African American, she understood deeply how hard it was for her and people like her to make an impact, so she dedicated time to educate and inspire Black students to pursue careers in medicine and the sciences long after her career began.

Marie Maynard Daly was born on April 16, 1921, in Queens, New York. She attended an all-girls school, Hunter College High School, where she developed her dream of becoming a chemist. Her passion for science was inspired in part by her father, who had started his chemistry degree at Cornell University but had to drop out due to financial issues.

Daly was determined to accomplish the goal. She began her undergraduate education at Queens College and graduated magna cum laude in 1942. Due to her stellar academic performance, the college offered her a position as a laboratory assistant in exchange for a graduate fellowship to study chemistry at New York University, where she earned her master's degree in one year.

Then, in just three years, Daly achieved her PhD in chemistry from New York University, becoming the first African American woman in U.S. history to earn the distinction. Daly researched digestive enzymes and the process of digestion in the human body.

Daly spent many years of her professional life teaching and instructing. After earning her doctorate, she taught at Howard University and later taught biochemistry at Columbia University. She spent several years working for the American Cancer Society researching cell nuclei. Her research contributed greatly to the later discovery of **DNA** in the early 1950s. She also performed pivotal research in cardiac health by studying **hypertension** and **cholesterol**, and her researched helped lay the groundwork for common benchmarks and practices for physicians all around the world assessing heart health in their patients.

Throughout her career, Daly witnessed the lack of women and racial minorities in research and medical positions, so she dedicated much of her time to educating and inspiring Black youth to pursue careers in medicine and the sciences. She even created a scholarship fund at her alma mater to support such students studying for graduate degrees in the sciences. Marie Maynard Daly passed away on October 28, 2003, but her contributions to medicine and the field of chemistry have left a legacy that will not be forgotten.

YURI KOCHIYAMA was a Japanese American woman who suffered from racial injustice and discrimination and used her experiences as a catalyst to fight for change. She lived through many pivotal moments in American history, and she leveraged her power and passion to consistently confront oppression, even if it wasn't directly affecting her.

Yuri Kochiyama was born on May 19, 1921, in San Pedro, California, to two Japanese immigrant parents. She spent her childhood living in a predominantly white area, attending church and Sunday school, and going to a local high school where she was involved in extracurricular activities. In 1939, she began at Compton College, where she studied English and journalism, and she graduated in 1941.

On December 7, 1941, Japanese fight planes bombed the naval base at **Pearl Harbor**, killing thousands and prompting the **United States** to enter **World War II**. This event changed the lives of everyone in America, but **Japanese Americans** immediately felt pressure and judgment from the wider population, with many assuming they supported or somehow helped the Japanese attack. With the development of **President Franklin D. Roosevelt's Executive Order 9066**, Japanese Americans all over the country were being detained and sent to internment camps.

Kochiyama and her family were sent to a camp in **Arkansas**. She was without her father, who was in a hospital recovering from surgery around the time of the attack.

Hospital staff labeled him as a prisoner of war, and he died shortly after. These traumatic experiences inspired Kochiyama to dedicate her life to fighting social injustice.

After she was released from the camp, she moved to **Harlem** in New York City, where she became involved civil rights causes for many minorities, including Latino, African American, and Asian American groups. Kochiyama believed that all minorities were similarly and collectively oppressed, and that they could work together to fight for their civil rights and end discrimination. Through her work, Kochiyama became close friends with radical activist **Malcolm X**, who often condoned and supported violence during the **Civil Rights Movement**.

This friendship directed Kochiyama into a more radical style of activism. She was watched and documented by the Federal Bureau of Investigations (FBI) for her involvement in the Civil Rights Movement. A lot of her activism focused on supporting and gaining compensation for political prisoners—something else she also experienced.

Kochiyama passed away on June 1, 2014, but she left a legacy that many still fighting for equal opportunity and treatment still hold close. She was known as a **human rights activist** who truly cared about all humans, involving herself in the plight and struggle of people of differing backgrounds, understanding that these differences didn't need to separate them, but they could unite them in a common fight for justice.

MAMIE TILL forced the world to acknowledge racism and discrimination in the wake of her son's gruesome murder in August 1955. Her determination to confront the evil sowed into American society and to fight for decades inspired oppressed peoples everywhere to stand up for themselves.

Mamie Till was born on November 23, 1921, in the small town of Webb, Mississippi. Soon after Mamie was born, her father moved the family out of the volatile American South and away from work in the cotton fields. They settled just outside of Chicago, Illinois.

Till's mother and father divorced when she was young, but her mother remained strict, demanding Till behave and focus on her studies. She made the honor roll and was one of the first Black graduates from her high school.

At eighteen, she met her future husband, Louis Till, and the year after they married, Mamie gave birth to their son, **Emmett Till**, in 1941. A few years later, Mamie and Louis separated, and Louis was shipped off in the war and later killed, leaving Mamie as a single parent to raise Emmett on Chicago's South Side.

One summer, Till was leaving the area to visit relatives in Nebraska, but Emmett wanted to join his cousins to visit distant relatives in Mississippi. On August 28, 1955, Emmett Till was murdered by a group of white men who were angry about him speaking to a white woman working at a grocery store days earlier. The men brutally murdered Emmett and tossed his body into the Tallahatchie River; his body was discovered swollen and disfigured days later.

When Till received the news, she demanded her son's body be brought back to Chicago. She then stunned the nation when she chose to leave his casket open at his funeral so others could see what had been done to her son. The gruesome fate he experienced was undeniable to everyone who attended his services. The murder drew international attention and put America's civil rights issues in the spotlight. Emmett's murderers were acquitted by an all-white jury, and the verdict caused an uproar around the world.

Although she was hurt and angry, in the wake of Emmett's murder, Till launched herself into activism and outreach. She toured across the country to speak to crowds and inspire them to fight back for their rights. She shared her extraordinary experience and used it to connect and motivate oppressed African Americans all over the nation. In 1957, she married Gene Mobley, who had been a friend and father figure to Emmett before he was murdered, and she changed her surname to Till-Mobley.

Till-Mobley's bravery and stoicism was an early seed of the Civil Rights Movement when others were inspired to stand up and make their voices heard. After decades of service to social justice and the efforts to end discrimination in America, Till-Mobley passed away on January 6, 2003, at the age of eighty-one in Chicago, Illinois.

◆ "Shark Lady" **EUGENIE CLARK** explored the seas and the oceans to give humans a better awareness of life underwater. She worked to improve the public's opinion of sharks and build understanding of the creatures. Working as a marine biologist and conservationist, she challenged perceptions that women, and specifically Asian American women, couldn't find success or make an impact in the sciences.

Eugenie Clark was born on May 4, 1922, in New York City, to a Japanese mother and American father. From a young age, Clark was obsessed with the ocean and its animals. She spent many days in the New York Aquarium observing fish.

After graduating from high school, Clark decided to pursue **ichthyology**, a type of biology focused on fish. Many people tried to convince Clark that she should pursue a more traditional career better suited for women at the time, but she refused and followed her passion of sea life. She attended Hunter College for her undergraduate degree and New York University for her PhD. In the mid-1940s, she became a research assistant at Scripps Institution of Oceanography in California, where she learned to scuba dive—a skill she'd use throughout her entire career.

In 1947, she faced discrimination when the U.S. Fish and Wildlife Service requested that she study the sea in the Philippines, but the FBI detained her because they thought her Japanese background was suspicious. Clark did not let this stop her from pursuing her interests and passion, though. In 1949, she was given the opportunity to travel to the Red Sea in Egypt, an area that had been mostly unexplored up until that point. After her adventures, Clark published the book *Lady with a Spear*, which became a bestseller around the world.

Clark discovered many fish species over the span of her career, but she is most remembered for her work to understand and advocate for **sharks**. At the time, most of the world believed sharks were unintelligent predators who were aimlessly violent toward other creatures, but Clark wouldn't accept that misconception.

Known affectionately as "Shark Lady," she performed pivotal research on several species of sharks. Her findings dispelled myths that sharks lacked intelligence, and she worked hard to rewrite the narrative that people should dislike them or be afraid of them.

Clark continued exploring the ocean until the end of her life. She performed her last ocean dive at the age of ninety-two before she passed away in Sarasota, Florida, on February 25, 2015.

◆ A member of the **Blackfoot Confederacy**, **MINNIE SPOTTED WOLF** made history when she enlisted in the **United States Marine Corps Women's Reserve** amid **World War II**. She became the first **American Indian** woman to enlist in U.S. history, showcasing the drive and heart of indigenous people in service to their communities.

Minnie Spotted Wolf was born in 1923 near Heart Butte, Montana. She was born a member of the Blackfoot Confederacy. She spent her childhood doing grueling work on her father's ranch. She drove large trucks, trained horses for riding, and cut fence posts—which were very physical jobs.

Spotted Wolf credited her time on her family's ranch with preparing her for her biggest adventure—enlisting in the Women's Reserve. She became the first American Indian woman to enlist in 1943. She initially showed interest in the military right at the start of the United States' involvement in World War II in 1941. However, when she visited a recruitment officer, he told her the war was not for women. Just a couple of years later, she joined the Women's Reserve.

During her time in boot camp at Camp Lejeune in North Carolina, she gained fifteen pounds from the intense exercise. Spotted Wolf spent her time in the Women's Reserve as a heavy equipment operator and a driver, working on bases in California and Hawaii. Her time as an enlisted woman drew attention from the public, and she was featured in media coverage in hopes of promoting involvement in the war effort.

Spotted Wolf served for four years in the military. After her service, she returned home to Montana and pursued a degree in elementary education. She worked as a teacher for nearly three decades before passing away on January 1, 1988, at the age of sixty-five. Even after many years

removed from her military service, she still honored that time in her life and the barrier she crossed by serving. She was buried in her military uniform. In 2019, U.S. Route 89 was dedicated in her honor as the "Minnie Spotted Wolf Memorial Highway." Her legacy is an inspiration to minority women as an exceptional case of being able to overcome the assumptions and words of others and know one's limits.

One of only two Chinese American women to be admitted to the prestigious WASP program during World War II, **MAGGIE GEE** was a third-generation Chinese American who was enamored with aviation as a young girl. She pushed through racism, sexism, and discrimination to realize her dream of being a pilot and contributing to America's war effort. Her steadfast determination positioned her as a role model for Asian American women working to move past societal barriers to success and recognition.

Maggie Gee was born on August 5, 1923, in Berkeley, California, as one of six siblings. Discrimination toward **Chinese Americans** was growing around the time Maggie was born, so much of her childhood was spent confronting those challenges.

At a young age, Gee fell in love with planes and aviation, often visiting the nearby Oakland Airport to watch planes fly in and out. One of her fondest childhood memories was when she spotted **Amelia Earhart**, and the two exchanged waves.

With the start of **World War II**, opportunities for women in aviation opened up. After saving money and taking pilot lessons in Texas, Gee applied to join the **WASP**. Very few applicants were accepted, but she was one of them. She and **Hazel Ling Yee** were the only two Chinese American WASPs.

One of Gee's duties as a WASP pilot was to assist in gunner practice. She would fly planes towing targets for shooters to practice on, and they'd fire live ammunition as she flew, making the responsibility incredibly dangerous.

The WASP program was disbanded on December 20, 1944, with the end of the war looming. Many women who survived their time as WASPs returned to caring for their homes and families, but Gee wanted something different. She returned to California and finished her degree at the University of California, Berkeley where she studied **physics** and **math**. After graduating, she worked on weapons systems at the Lawrence Livermore National Laboratory. She trailblazed a successful career for herself as a research physicist, which was a very uncommon career for not only Asian American women but all women in general at the time.

Maggie Gee passed away on February 1, 2013, in Oakland, California, at the age of eighty-nine. Before her death, in 2009, she worked to ensure that all living WASPs were awarded the **U.S. Congressional Gold Medal** for their service in **World War II**.

CORETTA SCOTT KING worked to honor her late husband's legacy after his assassination, but through her work, she solidified her own legacy as a human rights activist and a renowned author. Thrust into the national spotlight as a young mother and wife, Coretta dedicated her life to confronting injustice and promoting quality, even when it meant her safety and security were threatened.

Coretta Scott was born on April 27, 1927, in Marion, Alabama, as one of four children. Both her parents were ambitious, and their attitudes imprinted on Coretta. Coretta showed great musical ability from a young age, and she had a beautiful voice. She was the lead in her grade school choir, and she went on to be named valedictorian of her high school class.

She graduated from Antioch College in Ohio with a degree in music—where she first became involved in the Civil Rights Movement—before earning a scholarship to the New England Conservatory of Music in Boston, Massachusetts, in 1951. While Coretta was studying there, she met her future husband and iconic civil rights activist **Martin Luther King Jr.**, who was studying theology at Boston University. By 1953, the pair were married, and they moved to **Montgomery, Alabama**, so Martin could work as a pastor of the **Dexter Avenue Baptist Church**, a location that would fuel the early sparks of the **Civil Rights Movement**.

As the movement picked up steam in the mid-1950s, the Kings were thrust into the spotlight as leading activists of the movement. Coretta remained strong as her home was regularly targeted by white supremacists while her children slept inside, and her husband was away gathering support for their cause. She was also openly critical of the Civil Rights Movement not including women in the efforts.

After her husband's assassination in 1968, Coretta remained a prominent figure in the movement. Just after his death, she participated in labor marches, and she was heavily involved in the **women's movement**.

In 1968, Coretta founded the **Martin Luther King Jr. Center for Nonviolent Social Change** (now commonly known as the King Center) in Atlanta, Georgia, a nonprofit organization with the mission of promoting peaceful dialogue and change for the betterment of all society.

Coretta worked to uphold her husband's legacy for the rest of her life. She died on January 30, 2006, at the age of seventy-eight. She was buried alongside her late husband in Atlanta. Her headstone quotes 1 Cor. 13:13: "And now these three remain: faith, hope and love. But the greatest of these is love."

The first **Asian American** woman elected to **U.S. Congress, PATSY MINK** overcame persistent challenges due to her gender and race in order to serve people who were facing similar circumstances. Her example broke barriers for other Asian American woman wishing to pursue careers in law, politics, and public service.

Patsy Mink was born on December 6, 1927, in Paia, **Hawaii**. Mink was born as a third-generation **Japanese American**. In high school, she was elected vice president, and she received high marks and graduated valedictorian of her class.

She attended Wilson College in Pennsylvania and then the University of Nebraska. However, she soon transferred after witnessing the school's discriminatory practices of separating minority students from white student dorms. Eventually, she returned to Hawaii to finish her education at the University of Hawaii. In 1948, she graduated with a degree in zoology and chemistry, and she had high hopes for a degree in medicine.

She applied to a dozen medical schools and was rejected by all, so she changed her career path to law. In 1951, she graduated from the University of Chicago Law School. Patsy married and returned to Hawaii and sat for the bar exam, but it was difficult for her to find a job due to judgments from her **interracial marriage**.

Mink was determined to not let discrimination limit her life opportunities. She decided to open her own law firm, becoming the first Japanese American attorney to practice law in the state of Hawaii. In 1959, Hawaii officially became part of the United States, and Mink immediately began campaigning for U.S. Congress. She failed to be elected, but she was not discouraged.

In 1962, Mink was elected to a seat in the Hawaii State Senate, but she never took her eyes off a seat in Congress. Two years later—after an incredible effort by herself, her husband, and many volunteers—Mink won a seat in the **U.S. House of Representatives**, crowning her as the first Asian American woman elected to U.S. Congress.

Mink served in Congress from 1965 until 1977, then again in 1990 after winning a special election seat. She spent her time in politics working to improve the lives of minorities and people of lower socioeconomic status. She cared deeply about correcting race and gender inequalities. Her most shining achievement was her authoring of the **Title IX Act**, which required equal funding for women's academic and athletic programs in federally funded institutions.

Mink worked in civil service and politics until the end of her life. She passed away on September 28, 2002, in Honolulu, Hawaii, after battling pneumonia. Her name was still on the ballot for reelection that November, and constituents elected her in a landslide victory, even though another candidate would have to serve in her place. After her death, Title IX was renamed to the Patsy Takemoto Mink Equal Opportunity in Education Act.

The world's first African American tennis champion, **ALTHEA GIBSON** helped to break through the racial barrier that prevented Black Americans from competing in sports, and she paved the way for later tennis greats like Arthur Ashe and Venus and Serena Williams.

Gibson was born in South Carolina into a family of poor sharecroppers. As a child, she and her family—eventually growing to four girls and one boy—moved to New York City's Harlem, where they lived in a very small tenement apartment. Gibson, who described her childhood as "restless," spent much of her time in the streets, playing hooky from school and eventually dropping out of high school. Although she had a series of jobs, she was unable to keep them for long.

Gibson's first contact with tennis came through the game of paddleball, which she quickly mastered, and her natural skill caught the attention of a local coach who gave Gibson her first tennis racket. In 1941, just one year after she had her first tennis lesson, Gibson won the New York State Negro Girls' Singles Championship, and in 1945, she won the **National Negro Girls Championship**. Gibson would eventually win nine consecutive national championships for Black women players.

Despite her success, Gibson was barred from competing in major tennis tournaments against white opponents. She gained an important supporter in retired tennis star **Alice Marble**, who helped pressure officials of the National Grass Court Championships at Forest Hills in New York to let her compete.

In 1950, Gibson became the first African American permitted to play in this prestigious event. The following year, she became the first African American invited to play at **Wimbledon**, England's world-famous championship. In 1956, Gibson won both the singles and doubles **French Open** titles; the next year, she would become the dominant women's tennis player in the world, winning the Wimbledon championship and the **U.S. Nationals** at Forest Hills (now known as the US Open).

After winning both titles again in 1958, and at the top of her game, Gibson shocked the tennis world by announcing her retirement. She felt she needed to earn a living, and at the time there were few opportunities for an amateur woman tennis player. That same year, Gibson published her autobiography, *I Always Wanted to Be Somebody.*

Gibson later embarked on a singing and acting career, but her love for sports proved irresistible. In 1963, she took up golf and became the first Black woman to qualify for the Ladies Professional Golf Association (LPGA). During the 1970s and 1980s, Gibson served as a tennis coach and a mentor to athletes, particularly young Black women. In 1971, Gibson was inducted into both the **National Lawn Tennis Hall of Fame** and the **International Tennis Hall of Fame**.

◆ As **First Lady** for one thousand days, **JACQUELINE "JACKIE" KENNEDY** earned the admiration of the country for her style and grace. As the grieving widow of a martyred president, she earned the respect and gratitude of a shocked nation as it struggled to cope with the tragedy of November 22, 1963.

Jacqueline Lee Bouvier was born in Southampton, New York, the daughter of a stockbroker father and a mother from a socially prominent New York banking family. After attending Vassar College and George Washington University, Jacqueline met **John F. Kennedy**, popularly known as **JFK**, while working as the "Inquiring Camera Girl," interviewing people and taking their photos for a daily column in the *Washington Times Herald*. The couple married in 1953, a year after JFK was elected to the Senate. Jacqueline slowly adjusted to her role as a senator's wife and actively participated in JFK's successful presidential campaign in 1960.

As First Lady, Jacqueline Kennedy set fashion trends with her clothes, hairstyles, and her famous pillbox hat that became a trademark. She directed a major restoration of the White House and gave the first televised tour of the mansion in 1962. She and the president also hosted numerous cultural events, featuring performances by such noted artists as cellist **Pablo Casals** and violinist **Isaac Stern**. When she traveled with the president, she was so popular with the public that, during one trip to France, JFK identified himself as "the man who accompanied Jacqueline Kennedy to Paris."

Jacqueline was riding with the president in the motorcade in Dallas, Texas, on November 22, 1963, when he was fatally shot by **Lee Harvey Oswald**. The First Lady supervised the arrangements for her husband's funeral and inspired a stunned and grieving nation with her strength and dignity. Her popularity continued undiminished after JFK's death, and a poll continually ranked her as the most admired woman in the world.

In 1968, Jacqueline shocked the country when she wed **Aristotle Onassis**, an enormously wealthy Greek shipping magnate twenty-three years her senior, with an extravagant lifestyle and a reputation for womanizing. The subsequent newspaper and magazine photos showing "Jackie O.," as the press dubbed her, living a jet-set life on Onassis's ships and in the Greek islands, added to the furor.

After Onassis's death in 1974, Jacqueline restored her public image when she moved back to New York City. There, she lived in quiet dignity, working as a book editor, raising her children, and guarding her family's privacy.

She also became active in charities and spearheaded the successful campaign to restore New York's Grand Central Station. Jacqueline Kennedy Onassis died of cancer in 1994 and was buried next to President John F. Kennedy in Arlington National Cemetery.

As one of the originators of *Sesame Street*, perhaps the most influential educational TV program in history, **JOAN GANZ COONEY** helped transform children's television programming in the United States.

Sesame Street was created to educate preschoolers, particularly those from disadvantaged homes, in basic number, language, and reasoning skills, while at the same time entertaining them with humor, music, snappy visuals, and the comical cast of proprietary Muppets. The show, which premiered on November 10, 1969, would eventually reach an estimated 235 million viewers each week in more than 140 countries.

Joan Ganz Cooney was born and raised in Phoenix, Arizona. After graduating in 1951 with a degree in education from the University of Arizona, she worked as a newspaper reporter before moving to New York City in 1954 to work in television publicity. In 1962, she began producing public affairs documentaries for the New York educational television station, winning an **Emmy Award** for her documentary *Poverty, Anti-Poverty, and the Poor.*

In 1966, Cooney was asked to prepare a report on how television could be better used to educate the very young. She saw in the assignment a great opportunity. "I could do a thousand documentaries on poverty and poor people that would be watched by a handful of the convinced," she recalled. "But I was never really going to have an influence on my times. I wanted to make a difference." Her report titled "The Potential Uses of Television in Preschool Education" demonstrated the educational value of television for preschoolers and became the genesis of *Sesame Street*.

With the help of funding from several foundations and the federal government in 1968, Cooney cofounded the **Children's Television Workshop** (**CTW**), bringing together top researchers, writers, teachers, animated cartoonists, and television producers. The group designed a program that would make learning the alphabet and numbers easy and fun by using the same techniques that made cartoons and commercials so successful—animation, songs, puppets, and humorous skits.

The success of *Sesame Street* led Cooney to produce other highly regarded educational programs that focused on building specific skills, such as reading (*The Electric Company*), science (*3-2-1 Contact*), mathematics (*Square One*), and geography (*Where in the World Is Carmen Sandiego?*).

Some critics have argued that the CTW technique of edutainment can lead students to expect the same kind of entertainment when they attend school. However, studies have shown that *Sesame Street* has had a positive impact on the learning skills of preschoolers. The program that Joan Ganz Cooney pioneered continued to be enormously popular into the twenty-first century and soon began entertaining the young children of many parents who grew up on the show themselves decades earlier. In 2007, the Sesame Workshop founded the Joan Ganz Cooney Center, whose mission is "To advance children's literacy skills and foster innovation in children's learning through digital media."

In 1981, **SANDRA DAY O'CONNOR** became the first woman to be appointed as an associate justice to the **U.S. Supreme Court** in its 191-year history.

Born in El Paso, Texas, Sandra Day O'Connor grew up on a very large cattle ranch on the Arizona–New Mexico border. When she wasn't in school, the young Sandra also learned to fix fences, ride horses, brand cattle, shoot a gun, and repair machinery. These activities endowed her with self-confidence and independence, and ultimately, they also influenced her character and future judicial temperament.

After graduating from high school, she entered Stanford University at the age of sixteen, and earned a degree in economics in 1950. She then remained at Stanford and received her law degree in 1952.

Despite having graduated third in a class of 102, she failed to win positions with law firms in San Francisco and Los Angeles because she was a woman. Indeed, she received only one job offer—but as a legal secretary. In 1952, she married her law school classmate **John Jay O'Connor**, and the couple worked as lawyers in Germany for three years. In 1957, they moved to Phoenix, Arizona, where O'Connor interrupted her law career for four years to raise their three sons.

When O'Connor returned to work, she entered politics, serving first as an assistant state attorney general, then as a state senator, and later a county judge. In 1974, she was appointed to the **Arizona Court of Appeals**, where she earned a reputation for making decisions protecting the rights of women, people experiencing poverty, and the citizens suffering from mental illness.

In 1981, **President Ronald Reagan** appointed O'Connor to the Supreme Court, in part because of her experience in all three branches of government.

O'Connor's service on the Court since her appointment was consistent with her confirmation pledge: "To do equal right to the poor and to the rich." She demonstrated her independent thinking on the Court, voting at different times with both conservative and liberal justices on important cases such as abortion rights, affirmative action, and censorship.

She was often the deciding swing vote in 5–4 decisions, which caused many to call O'Connor the most influential woman in America.

O'Connor's appointment to the Court helped pave the way for another woman to join the nation's most powerful judicial body. In 1993, President Bill Clinton appointed **Ruth Bader Ginsburg** (see no. 77) as the second woman Supreme Court justice.

In 2004, O'Connor wrote the majority opinion for one of the most closely watched Court cases in decades: the ruling that ordered the federal government to allow terrorist suspects held indefinitely to meet with counsel and to contest the charges against them in court. O'Connor retired from the Court in 2006 and was succeeded by Samuel Alito. In 2009, she was awarded the Presidential Medal of Freedom by President Barack Obama.

BARBARA HILLARY was the first African American woman to reach both **the North Pole and the South Pole**—an impressive feat. And what's more inspiring is that she did it in her mid-seventies. She showed people of all ages that their dreams don't have to slow down as they age, but rather it is important that we speed them up.

Barbara Hillary was born in New York City on June 12, 1931. She was raised in Harlem. Her mother had moved the family north from South Carolina in hopes of providing her children with a better education and future. Hillary took advantage of this sacrifice, and she stayed in school until she earned a master's degree in New York.

Her undergraduate and graduate studies were focused on **gerontology**, the study of the aging process. Hillary had an incredible career in nursing, focusing most of her time on educating and training people in how people age and how their care needs change as they grow older.

In her late sixties, Hillary was diagnosed with lung cancer. She survived the diagnosis, but a necessary lung surgery left her with only seventy-five percent of her original breathing capacity. Even still, she didn't let this impact her quality of life or sense of adventure.

After she retired from nursing, Hillary took a trip to Canada, where she photographed polar bears and developed in her heart a new love for the Arctic. In researching the region, she learned that no African American woman had ever reached the North Pole, so she set her sights on becoming the first to do so.

Hillary began raising money to fund her expedition, and in no time, she reached her $25,000 goal. To prepare, she hired a personal trainer to build her strength and endurance, and she took cross-country skiing lessons. On April 23, 2007, she became the first African American women to set foot on the **North Pole** at seventy-five years old. Most people would be satisfied with this historic moment under their belt, but Hillary wanted to keep going. A few years later, she set off again and became the first African American woman to reach the **South Pole**.

Outside of nursing and exploring, Hillary dedicated much of her time to serving her community. Before her landmark trips, she founded the Arverne Action Association, a nonprofit with the mission of improving the local neighborhood, and she also established *The Peninsula* magazine, where she also worked as editor in chief.

Her perspective shifted after her trips to the Poles, and she became incredibly invested in the fight to slow climate change. She began touring for speaking engagements to educate her audiences on the impact that humans have on the environment.

Barbara Hillary passed away on November 23, 2019, in Queens, New York, at the age of eighty-eight. Before her death, she made it a point to inspire younger generations to take advantage of all years of life—not just the youthful ones—and to never lose their sense of adventure.

◆ Known as a champion for marginalized people, **RUTH BADER GINSBURG** worked tirelessly to improve the lives of many—in particular women—while facing discrimination in her own field of law. She became the second woman and first Jewish woman appointed as associate justice to the **U.S. Supreme Court**.

Ruth Bader Ginsburg was born on March 15, 1933, in Brooklyn, New York, right at the end of the **Great Depression**. Her mother worked in a garment factory and her father was a fur dealer. From a young age, Ginsburg was taught to value education. She worked incredibly hard on her studies, but she was met with challenges along the way, including the death of her mother right before her high school graduation.

Ginsburg didn't let the tragedy slow down her dreams. She went on to study at Cornell University and graduated in 1954. She then married her lifelong sweetheart, Martin. Years later, after starting a family and living as a military wife while her husband served, Ginsburg was accepted into Harvard Law School, where she excelled in the rigorous academic environment. With only nine women in her five-hundred-person class, she regularly faced gender discrimination. Her husband was also studying at Harvard Law at the time, and when he developed cancer, Ginsburg attended and took notes for his classes as well, helping him stay on top of his own studies while receiving top marks for her own classes. Ginsburg also became the first woman member of the *Harvard Law Review*, a prestigious law journal.

The couple moved to **New York City**, and Ginsburg transferred for her last year of school to Columbia University. She graduated covaledictorian of the class of 1959. Even after clearly proving that she had exceptional talent in the field, Ginsburg found it hard to find a job because she was a woman. After graduating, she eventually found work as a clerk and was offered positions with various private law firms. She began teaching in 1963, and by the 1970s, she was heavily involved in **women's rights**, prompting her to work with the **American Civil Liberties Union (ACLU)**. Around this time, Ginsburg presented six **gender discrimination cases** before the U.S. Supreme Court.

In 1993, President Bill Clinton appointed Ginsburg to the U.S. Supreme Court. During her time on the court, she continued to fight gender discrimination, and she fought hard for both men and women who were being treated unfairly because of their genders.

Like her early life, she was still met with challenges throughout her career, but she did not miss a day of work on the bench. She was diagnosed with cancer five times, but she didn't let her illness or treatments keep her from serving the people of the United States.

Ruth Bader Ginsburg passed away on September 18, 2020, at the age of eighty-seven. She left an enormous legacy for younger generations to honor in their work to fight for equal opportunity for marginalized people around the country.

Feminist icon and poet **AUDRE LORDE** used her writing career to expose social injustices for many marginalized groups, including people of color, the LGBTQ+ community, and people living in lower socioeconomic classes. She is known for her raw and transparent approach to her experiences, and her work has helped many understand a different perspective of America.

Audre Lorde was born on February 18, 1934, in **New York City**. Both of her parents were immigrants from Grenada, an island in the Caribbean. She developed a love for **poetry** at a young age, and she began writing her own as a teenager. In interviews, she said that when she was asked questions or her opinion on a topic, she would often speak in poetry, reciting lines of memorized works that resonated with her.

Lorde studied at Hunter College, where she earned her master's degree in library science in 1961. She began working at a library and writing poetry in her free time. She published *First Cities*, her first published work, in 1968.

Lorde gained attention for her work, and she soon left her job as a librarian to facilitate poetry writing classes at the Tougaloo College of Mississippi. During her time there, she was exposed to the tumultuous **racial tensions in the Deep South**.

In 1970, she published her next volume of poetry called *Cables to Rage*, which focused on social injustice. It was also the first time she infused her poetry with **lesbian** themes. Lorde continued to have a very active writing career and published regularly. Although the focus of each of her volumes changed, she often wrote of experiences as a **woman of color**, **feminist**, **lesbian**, and **mother**.

Her writing provided readers with a radically new and rare perspective. She infused her art with commentary on race and gender inequality, feminism, and queerness. She fought against modern society's need to categorize people and assign them into specific identities. Above all, Lorde's writing was always transparent and personal; she shared intimate moments of her life and experiences, even when they weren't enjoyable or easy.

In 1981, Lorde, along with writers Barbara Smith and Cherrie Moraga, founded the Kitchen Table: Women of Color Press, whose mission was to support the work of Black feminists. The women felt that their work was not given due consideration or support by white authors, so they created their own platform.

Audre Lorde passed away on November 17, 1992, after a long and public battle with cancer. Before her death, she used the struggle as a way to connect with others by publishing *The Cancer Journals*. She left an incredible body of work behind her that continues to educate and inform generations on how to understand and support marginalized people in society.

No other person is more closely associated with the **women's liberation movement** of the 1960s and 1970s than **GLORIA STEINEM**. The founder of both *Ms.*, the only mass-circulation feminist magazine in America, and the **National Women's Political Caucus**, Steinem has been a key spokesperson for equal opportunities and expanded possibilities for women for nearly forty years.

Steinem was born in Toledo, Ohio, the daughter of a traveling antiques dealer father and a mother who was a journalist-turned-housewife. Her parents divorced before Gloria reached adolescence, and she lived in a run-down home with her mother, who suffered from severe depression.

Steinem graduated from Smith College and moved to New York City in 1963 to become a writer. One of her first magazine articles was "I Was a Playboy Bunny," which chronicled her undercover assignment working in a Playboy Club.

In 1968, she was a contributing editor for *New York* magazine and given the opportunity to write on political and social topics, including the burgeoning women's liberation movement and the issues that inspired it. In addition to her writing, Steinem became an advocate for feminism. She was both attractive and eloquent, with long blonde hair and always donning her distinctive aviator-style glasses. It is no wonder that she became a sought-after spokesperson for the feminist viewpoint.

In 1971, Steinem and a group of woman journalists set out to create a women-owned-and-operated magazine that would feature articles on women's subjects that they hadn't been able to run in the mainstream press. They named the magazine *Ms.*, after the form of address for women that was just coming into wide use and did not indicate a woman's marital status.

The publication avoided the traditional subjects of women's magazines—features on fashion, food, and domestic concerns—in favor of topics like "Raising Kids Without Sex Roles" and "Why Women Fear Success." Almost all 250,000 copies of the entire initial issue sold out in eight days. *Ms.* would become the most popular voice of feminism in America, and Steinem long served as its star and dominant influence.

In 1972, *McCall's* magazine named Gloria Steinem **"Woman of the Year,"** declaring that she had "become a household word" and "the women's movement's most persuasive evangelist."

Steinem never expected to marry, and she was "happy and surprised," when she and South African businessman **David Bale** wed in 2000. Regarding the marriage, Steinem said, "I hope this proves what feminists have always said—that feminism is about the ability to choose what is right at each time of our lives." Sadly, Bale died in 2004.

In 2005, Steinem cofounded the Women's Media Center alongside actress Jane Fonda and writer Robin Morgan. The organization's goal was to work "to make women visible and powerful in the media."

Congresswoman, teacher, and inspirational orator, **BARBARA JORDAN** was the first African American woman elected to Congress from a southern state.

Barbara Jordan grew up in the largest Black ghetto in Houston, Texas, the youngest of three daughters in a poor family. Her father, a Baptist preacher and warehouse laborer, taught her that race and poverty had nothing to do with her intellectual potential and her ability to achieve great things if she worked hard enough.

When a Black woman lawyer visited her high school on career day, Jordan decided that a career in law would be the best way she could make a difference. She studied at Texas Southern University, where she excelled at debate, and later received her law degree from Boston University in 1959. She was only one of two women in her law school, both of whom were Black women from Houston. After graduating, she began her law practice back in Houston, working at home from her parents' dining room table, and after three years, she finally earned enough money to open an office.

In 1962, Jordan decided to enter politics, running unsuccessfully for state legislature. After another failed attempt two years later, she finally won in 1966, becoming the first African American since the 1870s to serve in the **Texas Senate**, and the first African American woman ever elected to the Texas Legislature.

During her six years as a state senator, Jordan worked for social reform and cosponsored a minimum wage bill and a workers' compensation plan. In 1972, she became the second Black woman elected to Congress, following only Shirley Chisholm, and the first from the South.

Jordan rose to national prominence in 1974 as a member of the **U.S. House Judiciary Committee** that investigated whether President Richard Nixon was guilty of impeachable offenses in concealing presidential involvement in the Watergate scandal. In a stirring and memorable speech, Jordan justified her vote to recommend impeachment, declaring, "My faith in the Constitution is whole. It is complete. It is total. I am not going to sit here and be an idle spectator to the diminution, the subversion, the destruction of the Constitution."

In 1976, Jordan became the first African American to deliver the **keynote address** at a national political convention. Her eloquence and principled stances on tough issues caused one writer to observe, "Few members in the long history of the House have so quickly impressed themselves upon the consciousness of the country."

Jordan shocked her many supporters when she announced in 1977 that she would not seek reelection. Suffering from poor health due to leukemia and multiple sclerosis, which eventually caused her to rely on a wheelchair, Jordan left Washington to teach at the University of Texas, inspiring the next generation of public servants. In 1994, Barbara Jordan was awarded the **Presidential Medal of Freedom**.

When President Bill Clinton appointed **MADELEINE ALBRIGHT** to be **secretary of state** in 1997, she became the first woman to hold that position and the highest-ranking woman ever to serve in the U.S. government.

Albright was born Maria Jana Korbel in Prague, Czechoslovakia (now the Czech Republic). Her father was a Czech diplomat who fled to England with his wife and infant daughter when the Nazis entered their country in 1938. The family briefly returned to Prague after World War II, but they fled again in 1948 when the Communist Party assumed power. This time they emigrated to the United States, where her father became a professor of international studies at the University of Denver.

It was not until shortly after her confirmation as secretary of state that Korbel learned that she was a Czech Jew and not a Catholic as she had believed, and that three of her grandparents perished in concentration camps during the war. She responded to the discovery of her ancestry by saying, "I have been proud of the heritage that I have known about, and I will be equally proud of the heritage that I have just been given."

Korbel was interested in foreign affairs from an early age. "By the time I was eleven," she recalled, "I had lived in five countries and knew four languages. In my parents' home we talked about international relations all the time, the way some families talk about sports or other things around the dinner table."

In 1959, Korbel graduated from Wellesley College and married journalist **Joseph Albright**. Now an Albright, she moved with her family to Washington, DC, commuting from there to Columbia University in New York City to complete her PhD in international relations. Albright later became a professor of international affairs at **Georgetown University** in Washington, and director of the **Women in Foreign Service** program at the university's School of Foreign Service.

A respected foreign policy expert on Eastern European and Russian affairs, Albright served as an adviser to Democratic presidential candidates **Walter Mondale** in 1984 and **Michael Dukakis** in 1988. In 1992, President Bill Clinton named Albright **U.S. ambassador to the United Nations**, only the second woman to serve in that post.

During her four-year tenure as secretary of state, Albright won the respect of the international community for her straightforward, no-nonsense style, her in-depth knowledge of foreign affairs, and her diplomatic skills. She was a forceful and principled architect of U.S. foreign policy who helped to promote democracy around the world. In 2012, she was awarded the Presidential Medal of Freedom by President Barack Obama.

MILDRED LOVING hadn't intended to become a civil rights activist when she married her high school sweetheart at eighteen. However, when authorities arrested and charged the two for their interracial marriage in Virginia, she refused to sit quietly as one of her most basic rights was stripped from her.

Mildred Loving was born on July 22, 1939, in Central Point, Virginia. Mildred had a mixed background of African American, American Indian, and European heritage. Her town, Central Point, experienced an uncommonly peaceful coexistence of white and Black residents at a time when racial tensions were boiling over in many areas of the **South**.

Mildred met her future husband, a white man named Richard, while the two were in school. She attended an all-Black school, and he an all-white school. The pair fell in love, and when Mildred got pregnant, they decided to get married at the age of eighteen. The pair had to drive to Washington, DC, to get married because of **Virginia Racial Integrity Act of 1924**, which made interracial marriage illegal there. The two returned home to Virginia and began their happy lives together after marrying.

However, on July 11, 1958, Mildred and Richard were awoken in their bed and arrested for breaking Virginia's anti-miscegenation law. Someone had tipped off the police that the pair had wed. They were put in jail, with Mildred incarcerated for several days. Eventually, they pled guilty to the charges, and they had to leave their home state.

In 1963, just as the Civil Rights Movement was gaining momentum, Mildred wrote a letter to **Attorney General Robert Kennedy** to ask for his help. He directed them to the **ACLU**, who agreed to take on their case, *Loving v. Virginia*. The lawyers appealed the case, and it was eventually sent up to the U.S. Supreme Court.

On June 12, 1967, the **U.S. Supreme Court** unanimously ruled that Virginia's laws violated the **U.S. Constitution**. The Lovings and their children returned to their hometown. Mildred's determination to fight the injustice did more than improve her own life. This court ruling impacted all interracial couples in America as it outlawed any race-based restrictions on marriage throughout the entire United States.

Mildred, Richard, and their children lived happily until Richard's untimely death in 1975. Mildred passed away on May 2, 2008, after a battle with pneumonia. Several books and primetime movies have been developed to chronicle the couple's story and their bravery in fighting for their rights to marriage. Each year on June 12, many celebrate the unofficial **Loving Day** to honor the couples' accomplishment and the court decision that improved the lives of countless couples in America.

83 PATRICIA BATH

1942–2019

Known as the first Black female physician to receive a medical patent, **PATRICIA BATH** dedicated her life and career to the science of understanding and improving people's eyesight. Like many women and people of color pursuing scientific careers, she faced backlash from white male colleagues, but she didn't let them stop her from making history in her profession and improving the lives of people all over the world.

Patricia Bath was born in Harlem, New York, on November 4, 1942. Her father was an immigrant from Trinidad who worked on the city's subway system, and her mother worked as a housekeeper. Bath showed talent in the sciences in her youth, and when she was in high school, she received a grant to study **biomedical sciences** at Yeshiva University.

Her interest in a medical career was piqued, and she went on to receive her bachelor of science in chemistry, then a medical degree from Howard University. Bath went to New York University School of Medicine to study **ophthalmology**—a specialty that focuses on eye and vision health. She became the first Black American in residency there.

During her studies, Bath made a very important observation. She noted that in clinics with mostly white patients, blindness was only occasional, and in Black communities the frequency almost doubled. She began to realize that access to and education about healthcare was severely lacking in Black communities. Because of this, she proposed a new community outreach program for eye health volunteers to visit underserved community centers and nursing homes to help people fight eye disorders.

In the early 1970s, Bath took a position at the University of Los Angeles Medical Center, where she became the first Black American woman surgeon. She continued to contribute great research and knowledge to the discipline, but she was consistently met with discrimination, based on both her race and gender. She traveled abroad in the early 1980s to European institutions, most of which took her research more seriously than the American organizations she had been working with.

While working in Germany, France, and England, Bath developed a new technology for cataract treatment. On May 17, 1988, she received a patent for her invention—the Laserphaco Probe—making her the first Black American woman physician to receive a patent for a medical invention. At the time, this was the only option available to remove cataracts and restore optimal vision for patients all around the world.

Bath retired from the medical field in 1993, but she continued to spend her time educating and advocating for eye health, especially in underserved communities. She passed away on May 30, 2019, at the age of seventy-six, having left behind an incredible body of research and technological advances that improved the lives of thousands around the world.

Known as the "Queen of Soul," **ARETHA FRANKLIN** used her incredible gift of voice to uplift people of color fighting for equality in America. Her talent spanned five decades and inspired several generations of audiences.

Aretha Franklin was born on March 25, 1942, in Memphis, Tennessee, as the fourth of five siblings. Her mother was a gospel singer, and her father was a Baptist preacher. When she was ten years old, Franklin's mother died, and her father moved the family to **Detroit, Michigan**, where he accepted a job at a church.

From a very young age, Franklin loved to share her incredible voice. Many people who heard her sing thought that she was a child prodigy because she was mostly self-taught and because performing came so naturally to her. At fourteen years old, she recorded her first songs and performed with her father on his traveling sermon tours.

In 1960, she moved to New York and was pursued by record labels, eventually signing with Columbia Records and releasing her debut album *Aretha* in 1961. In this early part of her career, Franklin saw success, but a shift in the mid-1960s to a different label led her to churn out hit after hit, including classic songs like "Do Right Woman—Do Right Man," and "**Respect**." She won her first Grammy Award in 1967 for her work.

Franklin's commercial and chart success led to her being dubbed the **Queen of Soul**, but her empowering, soulful voice was also inspiring people in the ongoing **Civil Rights Movement**. During her childhood, her father was friends with **Martin Luther King Jr.**, and Franklin was asked to perform at his funeral. She was also tapped to perform at the **Democratic National Convention** that year.

Through the mid-seventies, Franklin continued to find success and explored and revisited many types of music styles, all of which her audiences and critics loved. However, with the emergence of disco and dance music, the popularity of her songs declined.

Franklin didn't allow the changing music and social landscape to keep her down, though. She continued to record music over the following decades, witnessing several resurgences in her popularity. Over the course of her career, she recorded more than forty albums and sold more than 75 million records worldwide.

In January 1987, she became the first woman to be inducted into the Rock and Roll Hall of Fame. By the end of her five-decade-long career, she had been nominated for forty-four Grammy Awards and won eighteen of them. Aretha Franklin passed away on August 16, 2018, at her home in Detroit, Michigan. Musical artists, civil rights activists, and many fans paid tribute to her contributions at her services.

BILLIE JEAN KING has been perhaps the single most influential figure in the successful fight for recognition and equal treatment of women athletes.

Billie Jean Moffitt was born and raised in Long Beach, California. Both of her parents were athletic, and as a child, she played football and softball. She took up tennis at the age of eleven, and just six months after taking her first lesson, she played in her first tournament.

Even as a youngster, she was noted for her aggressive, athletic play that seemed to clash with the then dominant image of the ladylike tennis player.

Billie Jean won her first tournaments at fifteen, when she captured the southern California girls fifteen-and-under championship and advanced to the quarterfinals of the national championship. In 1960, she reached the finals of the national championship, but lost to seventeen-year-old **Karen Hantze**. A year later, she teamed up with Hantze to win the women's doubles championship at **Wimbledon**. They became the youngest pair ever to win the prestigious event.

In 1965, Billie Jean married **Larry King**, who became her agent, business manager, lawyer, and adviser. The following year, she won her first Wimbledon singles championship. Over the next ten years, King won a record twenty Wimbledon titles: six singles, ten doubles, and four mixed doubles. During that time, she also won **four US Open singles** titles. In 1971, she joined the newly formed Virginia Slims tour and became the first woman athlete to win $100,000 in a single year.

In 1973, King accepted a challenge to play a $100,000 winner-takes-all match against long-retired former champ **Bobby Riggs**, who had boasted that a woman could never beat a man, even with a great disparity in age. Earlier that year, the fifty-five-year-old Riggs had beaten thirty-one-year-old **Margaret Smith Court** in a $10,000 match. This time, in front of thirty thousand people at the Astrodome and another forty million TV viewers, Riggs was soundly defeated as King crushed him in three straight sets.

King was a founder and president of the **Women's Tennis Association**, a union for players; a founder of tennis and softball leagues for professional women athletes; and a publisher of *womenSports,* a magazine that reported on the progress of women athletes in a variety of sports. In 1976, she helped to create **World TeamTennis**, a league of professional women and men in tennis. She was also the first woman to coach pro tennis players who were men.

Billie Jean King was inducted into the **Women's Sports Hall of Fame** in 1980 and into the **International Tennis Hall of Fame** in 1987. When she publicly came out as a lesbian in 1981, she was the first prominent professional woman athlete to do so. In the following decades, King became an advocate for the LGBTQ+ community and was awarded a **Presidential Medal of Freedom** in 2009 for her work.

A pioneer and icon in country music, **DOLLY PARTON'S** contributions to country music and entertainment are unmatched. She has set an example for others from humble beginnings, showing them that with passion, kindness, and authenticity, they can achieve more than anyone else before them.

Dolly Parton was born on January 19, 1946, in Locust Ridge, Tennessee, as one of twelve children. She grew up in a big musical family that struggled financially. Although times were sometimes tough, Parton found inspiration while performing at her church, which started her deep love for music.

Parton began writing music at a very young age, and she started touring locally to perform them at the age of ten. She continued to perform and write throughout her teenage years, and immediately after high school graduation, she moved to Nashville, Tennessee, to pursue her dream of making it big in the **country music** industry.

Early in her career, she partnered with Porter Wagoner who introduced Parton to the world on his show, *The Porter Wagoner Show*. The two performed together and shared several successful songs.

Later, Parton signed with RCA Records, and in the early seventies she produced two hits: "Joshua" and "Jolene." She was also known for her incredible **business sense**. From the beginning of her career, she made sure she owned all the rights to her music and recordings, which gave her complete control over her work and massive financial success that many artists of her caliber never get to enjoy. She had dozens of songs top several charts over her forty-plus years in the music industry, and she wrote more than five thousand songs.

Parton's fame began to stretch outside of the walls of country music when she started to take on acting roles. She made her film debut in the hit *9 to 5*, for which Parton earned an Academy Award nomination for her work on the film's soundtrack. In the early 1980s, Parton announced she was going to open her own theme park called Dollywood in Pigeon Forge, Tennessee.

When Whitney Houston recorded Parton's song, "I Will Always Love You," for the film *The Bodyguard*, it positioned her as one of the most successful songwriters in history on top of her own impressive vocal and performance talents.

Outside of her unmatched commercial and professional success, Parton is known as a compassionate **philanthropist**. As a strong advocate for children's literacy, she created **Dolly Parton's Imagination Library**, which sends free books to children all over the world every month, and by 2018, she had donated over 100 million books through the program. Other causes close to her heart include public health, public education, and scholarships.

An accomplished attorney, policymaker, and active political partner with her husband, **HILLARY CLINTON** redefined the role of America's **First Lady** before going on to serve in the **U.S. Senate**, the **Cabinet of the United States**, and eventually winning the Democratic Party's presidential nomination.

Hillary Rodham was born in Chicago, the eldest of five children in a conservative Republican family. While attending Wellesley College in the 1960s, she shifted her political views to the left and became a social and political activist.

After graduating from Yale Law School, she moved to Washington, DC, where she put her interest in the rights and welfare of children into practice by working for the **Children's Defense Fund**. In 1974, she served as a legal counsel to the House of Representative's Judiciary Committee investigating President Richard Nixon's involvement in the Watergate scandal.

In 1975, she married **Bill Clinton**, whom she had met at Yale, and in 1976, they moved to Little Rock, Arkansas, when Clinton was elected the state's attorney general. In 1978, Hillary became Arkansas's First Lady when Bill Clinton was elected governor. In 1980, she gave birth to their only child, a daughter named **Chelsea**.

As Arkansas's first lady, she chaired the commission to reform the state's educational system. She also became the first woman associate in Little Rock's Rose Law Firm, and in 1987 and 1991, she was named one of the one hundred most influential lawyers in the country.

When Bill Clinton became president in 1992, he appointed Hillary to lead a commission to draft a proposal for **national healthcare reform**. It was the most important policy role ever assigned to a First Lady. Although the healthcare initiative ultimately failed, Hillary earned respect for her expertise and ability. However, she continued to draw fire from those who were uncomfortable with her prominent role in the administration. During Clinton's second term, Hillary's support for her husband, despite the evidence of his infidelity that led to his impeachment, caused her popularity to reach an all-time high.

She began her own political career with her election to the Senate in 2000. She was the first female senator ever elected in New York and became the first former First Lady to serve in the Senate. She was re-elected in 2006. In 2008, she ran for the Democratic Party presidential nomination, but was defeated by Barack Obama, who went on to win the presidency. Clinton served as **secretary of state** during Obama's first term. However, she became the subject of criticism in 2012 when U.S. diplomats were killed during an attack on the embassy building in **Benghazi, Libya**. Many Republicans claimed that Clinton had not done enough to prevent the attack and that she did not respond to it properly.

In 2016, Clinton made her second presidential run. She won the nomination, becoming the first woman to win a major party's presidential nomination. Despite winning the **popular vote**, Clinton lost the election to Republican nominee Donald Trump, who won the presidential election in the **Electoral College**.

In June 1983, astronaut **SALLY RIDE** became the **first American woman in space**, when she spent six days in orbit as a flight engineer aboard the space shuttle *Challenger*.

Sally Ride was born on May 26, 1951, in Encino, California, and had dreamed of being an astronaut from childhood. However, she was also an outstanding athlete, and for a time, she had trouble choosing a career. Initially, she seemed headed for athletics, dropping out of college as a sophomore to pursue a professional tennis career. However, her love of science drew her back to academia, and in 1970, she gave up tennis and enrolled at Stanford University.

Ride graduated from the university in 1973, with a BS in physics as well as a BA in English literature. She remained at Stanford to earn a PhD in astrophysics, and was working there as a teaching assistant and researcher when she joined the astronaut program.

In 1978, the **NASA** accepted thirty-five candidates from more than eight thousand applicants; of the thirty-five selected, six were women—and one was Sally Ride.

Ride underwent an extensive year of training that included parachute jumping, water survival, gravity and weightlessness training, radio communications, and navigation. She also worked with the team that designed the fifty-foot remote mechanical arm shuttle crews use to deploy and retrieve satellites.

At age thirty-two, Ride became the youngest person ever to go into space. On her 1983 flight aboard the space shuttle *Challenger*, she took part in the deployment of two communications satellites and in the deployment and retrieval of the German-built Shuttle Pallet Satellite (SPAS).

Ride returned to space aboard the *Challenger* in October 1984, when she helped deploy the Earth Radiation Budget Satellite (ERBS). Fellow woman astronaut **Kathryn Sullivan** was also a member of the flight crew, and she became the first American woman to walk in space.

Sally Ride was scheduled for a third flight aboard the *Challenger* in the summer of 1986, but that mission was canceled when the spacecraft exploded shortly after takeoff in January of that year. Ride was the only astronaut selected to be a member of the special commission to investigate the tragedy and to recommend changes in the space program to prevent future accidents.

Ride left NASA in 1987 to resume her teaching career at Stanford's Center for International Security and Cooperation. Two years later she became director of the **California Space Institute**, a research institute of the University of California, and a physics professor at the University of California, San Diego (UCSD). In 2003, the *Columbia* disintegrated as it re-entered Earth's atmosphere, and Ride was asked once again to serve on the investigatory board.

Ride was a strong advocate for improved science education, and she authored several children's books about space. She died of pancreatic cancer at the age of sixty-one, and posthumously received a Presidential Medal of Freedom in 2013.

Marked as one of the most influential Asian Americans in modern history, journalist **HELEN ZIA** has dedicated her career to sharing the unique struggles that Asian Americans and all people of color experience in America today. Her writing and reporting led to much acknowledgment of injustices and major changes in policy and principles to improve society.

Helen Zia was born in 1952 in Newark, New Jersey, to two **Chinese immigrant** parents. She attended Princeton University in the early 1970s, and she finished her degree and graduated in the university's first-ever co-ed class. While there, she helped found the Asian American Students Association, which intensified her passion for her heritage and ensured Asian Americans received fair treatment in society. In the mid-1970s, Zia moved to Detroit, Michigan, where she held several labor-intensive jobs before realizing that she wanted to be a journalist.

When Chinese American **Vincent Chin** was murdered in June 1982 in Detroit, Zia's reporting on the case allowed for fellow Asian Americans to pursue justice for the racially motivated murder. She played a large part in bringing **anti-Asian violence** to the forefront of public dialogue in America and into the courtroom. She also provided pivotal investigative journalism on dating violence and date rape occurring at the University of Michigan, inspiring students and community members to organize and demand the school to introduce policy changes. Zia has focused much of her career on fighting homophobia, building and improving human rights, supporting feminism, and participating in antiwar movements.

From 1989 to 1992, Zia served as executive editor of *Ms.* magazine, a publication developed by Gloria Steinem (see no. 79) that featured commentary on feminist issues and the women's rights movement. Zia and her partner, Lia Shigemura, were one of the first same-sex couples to get legally married in California after the **U.S. Supreme Court** reversed a 1977 law banning it in May 2008.

Her first book, *Asian American Dreams: The Emergence of an American People*, was published in 2000 and received critical acclaim. Many of Zia's published works focus on the experiences and struggles that immigrants and minorities face while trying to build better lives and opportunities.

OLGA E CUSTODIO was the first **Hispanic woman to become a military pilot** in U.S. history. From the time she was a child, she dreamed of flying planes, but her early attempts at breaking into a career in aviation were hindered because she was a woman. She had to wait many years, but she finally got her opportunity to learn to fly with the **U.S. Air Force**, and she inspired many women who came after her.

Olga E. Custodio was born in **Puerto Rico** in 1953. Throughout her childhood, she moved often because her father was an officer in the U.S. Army. She lived in places all over the world, including the United States, Taiwan, Paraguay, and Iran.

The family returned to their native Puerto Rico when her father retired, and Custodio was able to graduate from high school there. She started college at sixteen years old, attending the University of Puerto Rico.

Her father's career inspired her to go into the military, and specifically to become a pilot, but she was challenged early on. She attempted to join her school's **Reserve Officers' Training Corps (ROTC)**—a program available at many colleges and universities throughout the United States to prepare students for careers as military officers. However, only men were permitted by the rules of the time.

Upon graduation, she worked as an accountant and met her husband. The family moved to Panama when Custodio was offered a job with the **Department of Defense**, and it was there that her dreams of flying would become a reality.

She applied to the U.S. Air Force and was accepted as a pilot candidate for the Air Force Officer Training School. She eventually became a flight instructor, becoming the first woman T-38 (a supersonic jet) pilot instructor. Custodio retired from her regular position in 1987, and then she joined the **U.S. Air Force Reserves**, where she served for another sixteen years. She retired from the military with the rank of Lieutenant Colonel.

After her military career, Custodio accepted a position at **American Airlines** as a commercial pilot. The career change meant that she was the first Hispanic woman to work as a commercial pilot for the company. She worked for the airline, flying regular routes all over the world, until 2008.

In her retirement, Custodio has pursued many passion projects, including mentoring and inspiring Latino youth who have an interest in aerospace careers. She is a member of the Hispanic Association of Aviation and Aerospace Professionals (HAAAP) as well as Women in Aviation International (WAI).

◆ A trusted voice for **Hispanic Americans**, journalist **MARÍA ELENA SALINAS'S** intense, fast-paced communication style catapulted her through a thirty-plus-year career in the news industry. She earned the faith and confidence of Hispanic Americans in her authentic, well-rounded storytelling, and she opened up doors for future Hispanic journalists to continue to tell their stories.

María Elena Salinas was born in **Los Angeles**, **California**, on December 30, 1954, to **Mexican immigrant** parents. After attending UCLA, Salinas began working as an anchor and reporter for a **Univision** affiliate in Los Angeles.

Seven years later, she started working as the anchor of *Noticiero Univision*, a nationally televised, Spanish-language evening news program. She also worked on *Aquí y Ahora*, a Spanish-speaking program featuring special investigative reporting. She has interviewed prominent figures all over the world, including every **American president** since Jimmy Carter. She has also moderated U.S. presidential debates, representing the interests of Hispanic Americans on the national and global stage.

Salinas spent thirty-seven years working with the Univision network. She became the most well-known Hispanic journalist working in the United States, and a trusted voice and messenger for her community. After her time at the Spanish-language network, Salinas moved to CBS.

Salinas was ready for a challenge and a new adventure. She wanted to report in English to new audiences and on new platforms. She brought a new focus to the power of the Latino vote in America in electing leadership. She has earned many accolades, including a Peabody Award, a Walter Cronkite Award for national investigative journalism, and a Lifetime Achievement Award from the National Academy of Television Arts and Sciences.

Outside of Salinas's live news reporting, she found great success as a news writer and radio host as well. Her column is syndicated across the United States, and it is published in both Spanish and English. Salinas has also felt a responsibility to use her success and platform to educate and motivate younger Latino generations. She cofounded the **National Association of Hispanic Journalists (NAHJ)** in 1984 to support growth and opportunity for Hispanic journalists working in America. Her work has promoted peace, tolerance, and transparent reporting to build understanding across communities.

In 1992, scientist, physician, and entrepreneur **MAE CAROL JEMISON** became the first African American woman in space when she served as a science mission specialist during an eight-day voyage on the space shuttle *Endeavor*.

It was a great achievement for a remarkable individual, which Jemison put into perspective by stating, "There have been lots of other women who had the talent and ability before me. I think this can be seen as an affirmation that we're moving ahead. And I hope it means that I'm just the first in a long line."

Mae Carol Jemison was born in Decatur, Alabama, and raised in Chicago, where her family moved for better educational opportunities for Mae and her two siblings. As an adolescent, Jemison was a fan of science fiction books, movies, and television programs, particularly the TV series *Star Trek*. It was, in Jemison's words, "one of the few programs that actually had women in exploration and technology roles. It also showed people from around the world working together. . . . It gave a real hopeful view of the universe and of the world, and how we might become as a group of people, as a species."

After graduating from high school in 1973 at the age of sixteen, Jemison attended Stanford University, where she pursued a double major in chemical engineering and African and Afro American studies.

Jemison earned her medical degree from Cornell University in 1981, after having served as a medical volunteer in Cuba, Kenya, and in a Cambodian refugee camp in Thailand. She completed her internship and then worked as a general practitioner in Los Angeles. In 1983, she joined the **Peace Corps** as a medical officer for Sierra Leone and Liberia in West Africa.

Jemison applied for **NASA's astronaut program** in 1986 and was one of fifteen selected out of two thousand applicants. After her extensive training program, Jemison finally took off into space with six other astronauts aboard the *Endeavor* in 1992. On board, Jemison conducted experiments on motion sickness and the impact of weightlessness on bone density and the development of frog eggs.

In 1993, Jemison resigned from NASA to concentrate on teaching, working on behalf of healthcare issues, and encouraging increased participation in science and technology by students of color.

Jemison joined the faculty at **Dartmouth College** and established the **Jemison Group**, a company that researches, develops, and markets space-age technology. Mae Jemison has been acknowledged as an outstanding role model for women and African Americans for her achievements as a scientist, physician, astronaut, educator, and businessperson.

In 1981, a committee of architects, artists, and designers selected the winning design for a **Vietnam Veterans Memorial** in Washington. They chose the work of twenty-one-year-old **MAYA LIN**, who at the time was still an undergraduate student at Yale University. Her design of a V-shaped, black granite wall listing the names of the nearly sixty thousand men and women killed or missing in action in Vietnam was a striking and controversial conception that radically differed from heroic monuments of the past.

a monument honoring those who lost their lives in a war fought against the Vietnamese. Through the bitter debate, Lin held firm to her conviction that her design "does not glorify war or make an antiwar statement. It is a place for private reckoning."

Dismissed by some critics a "black gash of shame," Lin's design struck a special chord with veterans and the families and friends of the fallen who came to touch the names of loved ones and leave personal mementos behind. Lin had created, in the words of one admiring critic, "a very psychological memorial . . . that brings out in people the realization of loss and a cathartic healing process."

Maya Ying Lin was born in Athens, Ohio, the daughter of parents who had fled China just before the Communist Revolution of 1949. Her father was a ceramic artist and dean of the Ohio University art school, and her mother was a poet and professor of Asian and English literature.

As a student, Lin demonstrated an aptitude for both mathematics and art. She entered Yale University, where she studied architecture and sculpture, though her professors encouraged her to choose one discipline or the other. "I would look at my professors, smile, and go about my business," she recalled. "I consider myself both an artist and an architect. I don't combine them, but each field informs the other."

During the controversy surrounding her design for the Vietnam Memorial, Lin was subjected to racial and sexist slurs from those who felt that an Asian American woman was an inappropriate designer for

"The Wall," as it came to be called, has become the most visited monument in America, attracting more than one million people annually, a testimony to a great artist's simple but profound vision and conviction.

In 1986, Lin earned a master's degree in architecture and went on to design the **Civil Rights Memorial** in Montgomery, Alabama; the **Museum for African Art** in New York City; and a monument to commemorate women at Yale University. In 1996, Harvard University presented Lin with an honorary **doctor of arts degree**. Lin went on to design dozens of award-winning architectural projects and installations all over the country and world. She was awarded the National Medal of Arts in 2009 and the Presidential Medal of Freedom in 2016.

American-born, Pulitzer Prize-winning journalist **SONIA NAZARIO** witnessed violence and oppression as a young girl in Argentina. Instead of allowing that experience to intimidate her, she decided to use her energy and intelligence to educate and inform others of the struggles people were facing in different parts of the world.

Sonia Nazario was born on September 8, 1960, in Madison, Wisconsin. Both her parents were immigrants from **Argentina**, where they emigrated to the United States in 1960 before her birth. Her family moved to escape from Argentina's harsh government. However, Nazario spent her childhood time split between Kansas and Argentina until **Argentina's Dirty War** of the 1970s and 1980s pushed her to move to the United States permanently.

She knew from an early age she wanted to be a journalist. Her decision came after she learned that journalists were being murdered in Argentina for reporting truthfully on their government's behavior. She wanted to dedicate her life to fighting injustice through the written word and listening to people's stories.

Nazario earned a bachelor's degree in history from Williams College in the early 1980s; then she went on to earn her master's degree in **Latin American studies** from the University of California, Berkeley. After college, Nazario began a career in journalism working for the *Wall Street Journal*. She spent a decade reporting for the publication.

In 1993, she joined the writing staff at the *Los Angeles Times*. In 1998, she wrote a series for the *Times* that would earn her a prestigious **Pulitzer Prize**. The series, titled "Enrique's Journey," followed a young boy from Honduras who was struggling to locate his mother in the United States. The series was later developed into a full nonfiction book, and it became a national bestseller.

Nazario dedicated a lot of her time to covering the stories and experiences of immigrants, particularly Hispanic immigrants. In 2014, after she reported from Honduras to research and report on the circumstances in the country pushing refugees to the U.S. border, she was asked to provide her perspective on the crisis for the **United States Senate Committee on Foreign Relations**. She contributes opinion pieces, many on the topic of immigration, to the *New York Times*. Nazario also joined the nonprofit **Kids in Need of Defense (KIND)**, which provides legal services to immigrant minors who don't have guardians with them in America.

The focus of Nazario's reporting and storytelling have remained consistent over her career. Although events and circumstances change, she continues to acknowledge people who are challenged and held down by society, and she commits her time to telling their stories and doing her best to help improve their lives.

Vice President **KAMALA HARRIS** has dismantled many gender and racial barriers throughout her career. Although it was far from her first, her election as vice president in 2020 was one of the most powerful examples of breaking a **glass ceiling** that women and young girls around the world had seen to date.

Kamala Harris was born on October 20, 1964, in **Oakland, California**. Her mother was an **Indian immigrant** who had come to the United States in the 1950s; she worked as a biomedical scientist. Her father was a **Jamaican immigrant** who worked as a professor at Stanford University.

Harris attended Howard University, an **HBCU**, where she studied economics and political science. She went on to attend the University of California, Hastings for law school, where she graduated in 1989. After law school graduation, she worked in a district attorney's office as a deputy district attorney, which exposed her to a career in public law. She was elected district attorney in 2004 for San Francisco County, becoming the first woman to hold that position.

Harris made a point of breaking **gender barriers** throughout the rest of her career to date. In 2010, she was elected attorney general of California—the first Black American and first woman to do so. In 2012, she gained national attention when she spoke at the **Democratic National Convention**. In 2016, she became the first Indian woman and second Black American woman in U.S. history to be elected as senator for California. During her campaign, she fiercely supported protecting women's rights, reforming immigration practices, and working to improve the lives of working-class Americans.

In early January 2019, Harris announced that she was running for president. At the beginning of her campaign, she was seen as a serious contender, but later that year her support decreased, and she dropped out of the race in December. Although she failed to win the election, this opened another door for Harris's career.

In August 2020, Democratic presidential nominee Joe Biden selected Harris as his running mate and **vice-presidential candidate**. In November 2020, they won the election. On January 20, 2021, Harris became the first woman, Black American, and Asian American to be sworn in as vice president of the United States. While serving the nation in one of the highest positions, Harris has committed herself to serving the needs of working American families and setting an example for how to break social barriers.

TAMMY DUCKWORTH began her career in the military, becoming a hero after a tragic incident left her life changed forever. Duckworth used her experience to propel her into a life of public service after her military career ended, accomplishing many "firsts" in her service, including representing **people with disabilities** and **Asian Americans** in public service.

Tammy Duckworth was born on March 12, 1968, in **Bangkok, Thailand**. Her father was a U.S. military veteran who worked for the United Nations, so the family spent most of her childhood moving around Southeast Asia. When Tammy was sixteen, they relocated to **Honolulu, Hawaii**, where she finished high school.

She went to the University of Hawai'i at Mānoa to study political science and graduated in 1989. Then, she received her master's degree in international affairs from George Washington University. While studying for her master's degree, Duckworth decided to honor her family's legacy in military service, and she joined the **Army Reserve Officers' Training Corps**. Later, when she was in the National Guard, she decided to fly helicopters because it was one of the few combat positions open to women. Her doctoral studies were then interrupted, and she was deployed to help in the **Iraq War** in 2004.

While serving in Iraq, Duckworth suffered a life-changing injury. On November 12, 2004, she was flying her Black Hawk helicopter when Iraqi insurgents launched grenades at the helicopter. The crash caused her to lose both of her legs. While recovering from her injuries, she received the Purple Heart—one of the U.S. military's most prestigious awards presented to active-duty soldiers who have been hurt or killed while serving the country.

Duckworth used this experience to find a new purpose in life. After recovering, she began advocating for members of the military and became the director of the **Illinois Department of Veterans Affairs**, one of her first jobs in public service. In 2009, Duckworth was appointed by **President Barack Obama** as the assistant secretary of the U.S. Department of Veterans Affairs, where she was able to address veterans experiencing homelessness.

In 2012, she was elected congressperson to represent Illinois in the **U.S. House of Representatives**, becoming the first woman with a disability and first Asian American to serve in Congress for the State of Illinois. In 2016, Duckworth made history again when she was elected to the U.S. Senate. While serving as senator, she has made history as the first Thai American woman, the first woman with a double amputation, and the first woman to give birth in office.

Throughout her political career, Duckworth has prioritized veterans affairs and success. She uses her voice and presence to remind colleagues of the sacrifices that service members have made for American freedom. She has also served as a role model for women and other people living with disabilities. When she became the first woman to give birth while serving in Congress, she used her experience to start discussions on how to improve family-friendly work policies around the nation.

Known affectionately as "JLo," **JENNIFER LOPEZ** built a decades-long career and amassed immense financial success while serving as an icon in the **Latino community**. She has navigated a successful crossover career between music and film/television, proving that talent does not have limits. She infuses her work with her own authenticity and culture, and she has carved out a spaces for **Hispanic performers** to find success in the performing arts.

Jennifer Lopez was born on July 24, 1969, in **Bronx**, **New York**. Her parents were born in **Puerto Rico** and emigrated to the United States when they were young. Lopez loved performing from a young age, and she knew that she was meant for the spotlight.

She performed and won small parts at the beginning of her career, but in 1990, she got her first big break in show business when she won a spot as a dancer on the show *In Living Color*. Once the show ended, she moved on to other acting roles and gained national attention when she starred in *Selena* in 1997, a biopic following the life and death of the famous Mexican American singer. For her role in the film, she became the first Latina actress to earn more than $1 million for a film role. In the late 1990s, Lopez's music career grew when she released her debut album *On the 6*, which sold millions of records.

Lopez balanced successful music and acting careers—something many performers have found challenging. She has more than forty movie credits to her name, and she has released eight studio albums. She has been nominated for two **Golden Globe Awards**, which is one of the most coveted acting awards in the industry. She has received countless nominations and wins from prestigious music awards in the industry, including Billboard Music Awards, American Music

Awards, and World Music Awards. She has become one of the highest-paid Latina actresses in the entertainment industry. Many of her Latino fans have shared that her success positively motivated them to accomplish bigger things as well.

Lopez is also an incredibly successful businessperson and entrepreneur. She has signed to countless endorsement deals with existing megabrands like Coach and Designer Shoe Warehouse, more commonly known as DSW. She also has launched her own production company and lifestyle brands.

Lopez has used her platform to spotlight many causes close to her heart. She has supported or built programs advocating for childhood health and fitness, getting underserved communities access to healthcare, aiding disaster relief, and promoting gender and race equality.

One of the first two **American Indian** women elected to the **U.S. Congress**—and the first openly **LGBTQ+ American Indian** ever to be elected—**SHARICE DAVIDS** is providing a voice and path forward for many who have felt left out of mainstream politics and government.

Sharice Davids was born on May 22, 1980, in Frankfurt, West Germany (now Germany), while her mother was serving in the U.S. Army. Davids was born into the **Ho-Chunk Nation**, and several people in her family served in the U.S. Armed Forces.

Davids grew up in Kansas, and after graduating from high school, she earned her bachelor's degree in business administration before enrolling at Cornell Law School for her law degree. While pursuing her studies, Davids started pursuing an amateur and professional career in **mixed martial arts**. She trained for several years before deciding to focus her time on service and outreach for American Indian communities.

Davids began her law career working for an international law firm; then she shifted to a position supporting economic and infrastructure development on a reservation. In 2016, she worked under the Obama administration as a White House Fellow in the **Department of Transportation**.

In 2018, Davids decided to run for a seat in the **U.S. House of Representatives** to represent her home state of Kansas. She won the seat, and she was sworn in on January 3, 2019. Elected to the House at the same time as **Deb Haaland** of New Mexico, Davids was one of the first two American Indian women to serve in Congress and the very first openly LGBTQ+ American Indian to be elected.

Davids has been acknowledged by her peers and fellow LGBTQ+ as a trailblazer, who pursues social justice and equality for all people. She began her career in Congress, being named vice chair of the 2020 Democratic National Convention. She is chair of the **Congressional LGBTQ+ Equality Caucus** and the **Congressional Native American Caucus**—two groups focusing on legislative changes to support the two underrepresented groups.

Davids built her political platform on prioritizing accessible and affordable healthcare for all residents and restricting the influence of special interest groups on government leadership and decision-making. Davids's groundbreaking election to Congress illustrated to younger generations that people with diverse backgrounds and rich life experiences are not only able to reach the highest seats in government but also that it is imperative that they do so. Davids provides a voice for people who have had been given little acknowledgment or consideration in **American policymaking** in the past, and she is helping pave a better future for generations to come.

A **transgender rights** activist who has broken many barriers in the mainstream entertainment and media industries, **JANET MOCK** has built an impressive career in writing, journalism, directing, and producing, and she uses her position to tell stories that illuminate the experiences of the LGBTQ+ community.

Janet Mock was born on March 10, 1983, in Honolulu, Hawaii, as one of five siblings. Her mother was Hawaiian, Asian, and European, and her father was African American. Mock was assigned male at birth, but she stated that she knew from a young age that she was a girl stuck in a boy's body. By the time she was in high school, she started the process of transitioning. She named herself Janet after entertainer Janet Jackson, whom she saw as a role model.

Mock graduated from the University of Hawai'i at Mānoa in 2004 with a degree in fashion merchandising; then she moved on to study for her master's degree in journalism at New York University. She started working for *People* magazine right after graduation.

As she witnessed a rising suicide rate in the community, Mock wrote an article for *Marie Claire* in 2011 encouraging LGBTQ+ youth to find strength in their identity and hold true to who they are in difficult moments. In 2012, she signed on to write an autobiography about her experiences growing up as a trans person. The book, *Redefining Realness: My Path to Womanhood, Identity, Love, and So Much More*, was a *New York Times* best seller, and it provided much needed perspective and mentorship for **LGBTQ+ youth** all around the world.

Mock grew her career in the media industry, and she didn't confine herself to one path. She continued writing, serving as a contributing editor for *Marie Claire*, and contributed as a correspondent on MSNBC and *Entertainment Tonight*. She was featured on Oprah's *Super Soul Sunday*, and she was a speaker during the **2017 Women's March on Washington**.

Mock also added producer and director to her résumé when she developed the series *Pose* for the FX channel. This made her the first trans woman of color to both write and direct a television series episode for mainstream television.

Mock's commitment to honoring who she is while remaining authentic has allowed her to build a career that trans people all over the world can look up to and emulate. She not only followed her passion of communicating and creating content but she also found a way to leverage her talents to connect with people on a similar path.

The most decorated **gymnast** in American history, **SIMONE BILES** broke countless records in her sport. Her dominance on the world gymnastics stage serves as an example for women—especially women of color—that their strength and work ethic can take them anywhere. In 2021, she brought **mental health** conversations to the forefront, helping other young athletes and fans to be more comfortable confronting their own struggles.

Simone Biles was born on March 14, 1997, in Columbus, Ohio. Both her mother and father suffered from substance abuse issues, so Simone's grandparents adopted her and her sister, and they grew up in Spring, Texas.

At a very young age, Biles showed an interest in gymnastics. She started training at six years old. Her early coaches immediately noticed that she had very high physical and spatial intelligence without much training. Biles spent her childhood training at the same gym, and she won a gold medal at the Women's Junior Olympic National Championships in 2010. Immediately following this success, she entered the elite level of the sport.

Biles quickly became known as a top contender in the sport as she dazzled judges and peers with her expertise of all four events: vault, uneven bars, balance beam, and floor exercise. In 2013, she became the first Black American gymnast to win the all-around title at the **World Gymnastics Championships**. By 2015, she became the most decorated U.S. gymnast of the world championships in history after she totaled fourteen medals.

In 2016, she competed in her first **Olympic Games in Rio de Janeiro**. Biles and her teammates, known as the "Final Five," captured the team gold. Biles won gold in the women's individual all-around competition, vault, and floor exercise, and she received a bronze in the balance beam competition. In the years following, she continued to break records in the sport.

Biles's performance at the **2020 Olympic Games in Tokyo** (held in 2021 due to the COVID-19 pandemic) were highly anticipated. Shortly after competition began, she shocked the world when she withdrew from most of her team events and the all-around competition, of which she was a favorite to win. Biles and her coaches explained to the media that she withdrew after suffering from what those in the sport refer to as "the twisties"—a mental block that gymnasts sometimes experience, causing them to lose their spatial awareness after launching into the air, which can cause disastrous injuries. After undergoing medical evaluation and practicing away from the pressure of the public eye, Biles returned to competition a few days later, winning a bronze medal in the balance beam final. Biles used the circumstances as a springboard for discussing the unhealthy pressure placed on athletes, speaking out against the expectation that athletes should ignore their mental health in order to perform.

TRIVIA QUESTIONS

TEST YOUR knowledge and challenge your friends with the following questions. The answers are contained in the biographies noted.

1. Who was the First Lady who saved a famous White House portrait of George Washington before the British burned down the building? (See no. 6)

2. Which mid-nineteenth century astronomer discovered a comet that was subsequently named after her? (See no. 13)

3. What monopoly did Ida Tarbell help break up by writing her classic study of corruption in the oil industry? (See no. 19)

4. What field of science did Florence Bascom help pioneer? What did she specialize in? (See no. 26)

5. In what year did Jeanette Rankin become the first woman elected to the U.S. House of Representatives? (See. no. 35)

6. Where did Florence Price premiere her Symphony in E Minor? (See no. 39)

7. Who was the first Black actor to be nominated for or win an Academy Award? For what film? (See no. 44)

8. Whose work in the field of psychology was used in *Brown v. Board of Education* to help prove that segregation was harmful to Black children? (See no. 59)

9. What field did Eugenie Clark help pioneer? What is the nickname by which she is affectionately known? (See no. 67)

10. Who were the first two women appointed to the U.S. Supreme Court? (See nos. 75 and 77)

11. What important observation did Patricia Bath make in her patients? (See no. 83)

12. Who designed the Vietnam Veterans Memorial? (See no. 93)

PROJECT SUGGESTIONS

1. Choose one of the women from this book and write a one-page fictional diary entry for one day in that person's life. Pick a day that had some significance for the individual. For example, the day she achieved some long-held dream or goal, or the day she won a major award or received some official recognition. Alternatively, choose a day on which the person was met with a severe setback or was frustrated in some way by a lack of success. Describe the person's thoughts and feelings with as much detail as you can.

2. Arrange a "meeting" of two women in this book who could never have met in real life. Choose individuals from different eras, either from similar professions or walks of life or from completely different ones (for example, Emily Dickinson and Audre Lorde or Althea Gibson and Simone Biles). Imagine what their meeting would be like. Write one to two pages describing the scenario of their encounter and create a dialogue. What kinds of questions do you think they would ask each other? Would one approve of the things the other had done in their lifetime? Be as imaginative as you can.

INDEX

OUT NOW: